GETTING ON MESSAGE

GETTING ON MESSAGE

Challenging the Christian Right from the Heart of the Gospel

EDITED BY REV. PETER LAARMAN

BEACON PRESS / BOSTON

Beacon Press
25 Beacon Street
Boston, Massachusetts 02108-2892
www.beacon.org

Beacon Press books are published under the auspices of the Unitarian Universalist Association of Congregations.

09 08 07 06 8 7 6 5 4 3 2 1

This book is printed on acid-free paper that meets the uncoated paper ANSI/NISO specifications for permanence as revised in 1992.

Composition by Wilsted & Taylor Publishing Services

Library of Congress Cataloging-in-Publication Data

Getting on message : challenging the Christian right from the heart of the Gospel / edited by Peter Laarman.
p. cm.
Includes bibliographical references.
ISBN 0-8070-7721-6 (pbk. : alk. paper)
1. Modernist-fundamentalist controversy.
2. Liberalism—Religious aspects—Christianity.
3. Liberalism (Religion) 4. Christianity and politics.
5. Religious pluralism—Christianity.
6. Religious right. I. Laarman, Peter

BT82.3.G48 2006
273'.9—dc22 2005030608

CONTENTS

Introduction

PETER LAARMAN

Recently a small group of students from Occidental College in Los Angeles approached my organization, Progressive Christians Uniting, with the message that despite the college's deep commitment to diversity, there is literally no social space there for liberal Christians. Or as one of the students put it, "I am involved in all kinds of groups on campus that support social justice. Then one day it occurred to me that the reason I do all this is because of my Christian faith—so where is the Christian community on this campus that can support me?"

Thanks to the efforts of this student and others like her, there soon *will* be a progressive Christian presence at Occidental. But what an odd historical twist and what a commentary on the culture that even at our best liberal arts colleges, the only form of public Christianity on offer is what Rick Hertzberg and others have rightly labeled *Christianism:* an exclusivist creed that is fueled more by fear than by love.

The 2004 election and its aftermath—the Terri Schiavo drama, unprecedented attacks on the judiciary, the relentless advance of "intelligent design," and continuing assaults on gay equality and abortion—all bespeak a phenomenon that no one could have predicted. In the middle of the last century it was generally agreed that fundamentalism—a late and peculiarly American reaction to biblical criticism and to modernism generally—had been decisively defeated as a cultural force. Pundits assumed that it would live on in the South and in pockets of the Midwest but would never again pose a serious threat to enlightened liberalism and rational progress, let alone to core understandings concerning the separation of church and state. Thoughtful Christians would remain firmly committed to an ideal of secular, scientific progress. As education spread, the influence of primitive religion would dwindle almost to extinction.

It did not work out that way. In a classic demonstration of the Return of the Repressed, an old-style militant Christianity fusing superpatriotism, male supremacy, and rigid biblicism has reemerged as a potent cultural and political force in the space of five decades. This dramatic turnabout can rightly be seen as a brilliant feat of organizing on the part of a handful of conservative visionaries—and it certainly is that—but it can also be seen as a commentary on the spiritual vacuousness of the liberal project and as a rebuke of liberalism's inability to shield working people from the ravages of the corporate state. It can even been seen as an encrypted expression of white rejection of multiculturalism, despite the presence among the new Christianists of many leaders of color. There is room for many construals, each of them bearing part of the truth of what has happened.

Some of the essays in this book hint at the sources of the new Christianism that roils our politics, but the book is not intended to uncover the historical roots so much as deplore the practical effects. Many of the contributors to this volume—a diverse mix of preachers, thinkers, and activists along the moderate to progressive spectrum—fear that the message and meaning of Jesus have been all but drowned out by the noise machine of the Christian Right. Bill McKibben's essay puts this challenge directly: he ponders why nearly all public expressions of Christianity in America today bear little or no relation to what Jesus of Nazareth said and did. Reclaiming Jesus is a central concern for these essayists.

This book is also intended to take the Bible back from the blinkered biblicists and reemphasize the scriptural primacy of justice and mercy—what Marilynne Robinson in her essay calls generosity. Rather than take on the biblicists, many progressive Christians have simply walked away from the Bible. This is a strategic mistake inasmuch as tens of millions of Americans continue to respect and even revere the Bible's authority. But it is also a substantive mistake inasmuch as the heart and soul of the scriptural testimony is on the side of peace and justice. A plain reading will find Jesus and the prophets fiercely at odds with the kinds of social arrangements (notably rule by and for the wealthiest) now prevailing in the United States. The essayists represented here would have us reading the Bible more, not less, but would also have us doing so with a degree of sophistication and always with the caveat that Jesus Christ—his spirit, his generosity, his compassion—remains the true canon for faith and practice, which also means that anything "scriptural" that is *not* in accord with the spirit of Jesus cannot claim final authority.

I am convinced that there is a profound hunger in our culture now for the religion of Jesus—for a generous and compassionate Christianity that desires mercy, not sacrifice, and that actively pursues peace at every level.

In Southern California progressive Christians by the hundreds who have no church home have begun show up at the rallies and teach-ins presented by my organization. These are passionate, justice-seeking people who have not yet found a congregation that is sufficiently attuned to their own sense of urgency. They are outraged by the direction of the nation and by conservatism's suffocating grip on public discourse. If these "free radical" Christians could be organized to work in tandem with the millions of churchgoing progressives—and if both groups began to work strategically with enlightened secular forces in the culture—America's long night of conservative domination would be at an end. This is why seemingly sectarian and intramural struggles over what the Bible really says and who Jesus really is matter hugely to *all* progressives.

In France the idea that enlightened public policy might hinge on getting one's theology right would be laughable, but this is America. If moderate and progressive Christians can't get on message and get their act together, we will remain in a world of trouble (and let us remember that the Christianists *welcome* Armageddon). But if moderates and progressives *do* find a way to reclaim and express the heart of the gospel in ways that resonate, there may yet be hope for the democratic dream.

Out of the depths, life-giving progressive voices are beginning to be heard. That these voices should become a mighty chorus: that is my hope and that is the animating premise of this volume.

Hallowed Be Your Name

MARILYNNE ROBINSON

You shall be holy, for I the LORD *your God am holy.*

—*Leviticus 19:2*

I realize that in attempting to write on the subject of personal holiness, I encounter interference in my mind between my own sense of the life of the soul and understandings that are now pervasive and very little questioned The phrase, in what at present is its received sense, suggests a preoccupation with (usually) minor, nameable, and numerable sins and the pious avoidance of them where possible. It suggests a regime of pious behaviors whose object is the advantage of one's own soul. It suggests also a sense of security concerning final things that is understood as a virtue, though it is in fact a confidence not claimed even by the Apostle Paul. If this is a view of the matter commonly held by the unchurched and the irreligious, it is nevertheless a fair account of the thought and practice of many who do indeed aspire to personal holiness or who feel they have achieved it.

The approach to the issue I prefer is not original with me. It is neither less scriptural, less theological, nor less traditional than the sense of the phrase I sketched above, though it has gone into eclipse with the rise in this country of a culture of Christianity that does not encourage thought. I do not intend this as a criticism of the so-called fundamentalists only, but more particularly of the mainline churches, which have fairly assiduously culled all traces of the depth and learnedness that were for so long among their greatest contributions to American life. Emily Dickinson wrote, "The abdication of belief / Makes the behavior small." There is a powerful tendency also to make belief itself small, whether narrow and bitter or feckless and bland, with what effects on behavior we may perhaps infer from the present state of the Republic.

I believe in the holiness of the human person and of humanity as a phenomenon. I believe our failings, which are very great and very grave—after all, we have brought ourselves to the point of possible self-annihilation—are a cosmic mystery, a Luciferian disaster, the fall of the brightest angel. That is to say, at best and at worst we are within the field of sacred meaning: holy. I believe holiness is a given of our being which, essentially, we cannot add to or diminish, and whose character and reality is fully known only to God, and fully valued only by him. What I might call personal holiness is in fact openness to the perception of the holy, in existence itself and above all in one another. In other words, it is not my belief that personal holiness—sanctity, as the theologians call it—inheres in anyone in isolation or as a static quality. Acting with due reverence for the human situation, including the fact of one's own life, if that were possible, would be saintly. Instead we all struggle constantly with our insufficiency. To put the matter another way, we baffled creatures are immersed in an overwhelming truth. What is plainly before our eyes we know only in glimpses and through disciplined attention. Or again: to attempt obedience to God in any circumstance is to find experience opening on meaning, and meaning is holy.

I am speaking from the perspective of American liberal Protestantism. As I understand the history of this tradition, it departed in the mid-eighteenth century from the Calvinism its forebears had brought from England when it experienced the potent religious upheaval known as the First Great Awakening. The given of the movement was that people passed into a state of sanctity, and in effect were assured of their salvation, through an intense mystical/emotional experience, often a vision of Christ. The movement swept prerevolutionary America and left in its wake Princeton, Dartmouth, the temperance movement, a heightened sense of shared identity, and the model of revivalism as a norm of religious culture. There was criticism and reaction against extremes of enthusiasm and a significant Calvinist aversion to the idea that the fruits of salvation could be had by shaking the tree. Then there was a period of quiet, which ended with the onset in the early nineteenth century of the Second Great Awakening, again based on the belief that salvation was realized in a mystical/emotional experience. It swept the Northeast, sending zealous New Yorkers and New Englanders out into the territories, and helped to create the abolitionist movement, the women's suffrage movement, any number of fine colleges, a revived temperance movement, utopianism, Seventh-Day Adventists and Latter-Day Saints. And also a literature on the treatment of an affliction that was frankly called "religious mania."

Historically, mass religious excitements tend to be set off by plague and famine. These were set off by preaching, in the first instance by the Congregationalist minister and metaphysician Jonathan Edwards, first president of Princeton, and in the second by the Presbyterian lawyer and abolitionist Charles Grandison Finney, who went on to serve as president of Oberlin College. While both movements were remarkable for benign and lasting consequences, they left a heritage their own traditions rejected: the belief that salvation occurred in a discrete, unambiguous experience, which they called "conversion," and which those who have retained the belief call "being born again." An important criticism of this model was that it created misery and despair among those called the "no-hopers"—among whom Emily Dickinson found herself when a great revival swept through Mount Holyoke College. The liberal criticism—rejection of the idea that one could be securely persuaded of one's own salvation and could even apply a fairly objective standard to measure the state of others' souls—was in fact a return to Calvinism and its insistence on the utter freedom of God. That is to say, it was a rejection on theological grounds of a novel doctrine. So here has opened the great divide in American Protestant Christianity. And it must be clear from what I say at the outset that I fall on the liberal side of this division.

History is a great ironist, though historians seem rarely to see the joke. The first two Awakenings were the work of two Eastern intellectuals. Anyone who has read Edwards's "Sinners in the Hands of an Angry God," the sermon often said to have kindled in his church in Northampton, Massachusetts, the movement that spread through the colonies, knows that when he preached about damnation, he was preaching to the choir. That is, he did not encourage his flock to believe in their own special sanctity, nor did he encourage them to consider others to be in a more parlous state than they were themselves. Perhaps the whole great excitement passed as benignly as it did for that very reason. The excitement we are seeing now is called by some scholars a *Third* Great Awakening, yet it is different from the first two in this crucial respect. It is full of pious aversion toward so-called secular culture—that is, whatever does not give back its own image—and toward those whose understanding and practice of religion fails to meet its standards. If it is true that Edwards's movement unified the colonies, preparing the way for the Revolution, this may have been because his preachments encouraged people to believe that they themselves were their problem, not some hostile or decadent others who were corrupting the cultural atmosphere.

The Second Great Awakening, in which Charles Finney figured so prominently, was strongly focused on slavery and its abolition, and also on the education of women. Some part of its energies spun off into séances and experiments with marital arrangements, but in its main thrust it was profoundly progressive and reformist. It addressed inequality—of black and white, women and men, wealthy and poor—as social sin to be overcome, especially through greatly increased access to education. The movement we are seeing now is notably devoid of interest in equality. Indeed, it passionately supports a government whose policies have created a sharp rise in the rate of poverty. For a self-declared Christian movement, it shows startlingly little sense of responsibility for the vulnerable in society.

And here is the culminating irony. This movement, which calls itself fundamentalist, subscribes fervently to the principles of laissez faire capitalism. It has helped to push American society toward what the English economist Herbert Spencer called "the survival of the fittest." Darwin borrowed that phrase from Spencer to name the dynamic of natural selection in the evolution of species, otherwise known as Darwinism. In other words, our anti-Darwinists are Social Darwinists. The great defender of what were then called "the fundamentals" was William Jennings Bryan, a Democrat and a pacifist and a passionate campaigner against what he saw as the economic structures that created poverty. His

"Cross of Gold" speech spoke of the poor of America as Christ crucified —not at all the kind of rhetoric we hear these days. Bryan, a liberal by any standard, opposed Darwinism because it was taken at the time, rightly or wrongly, to justify not only economic exploitation but also racism, colonialism, eugenics, and war. He feared the loss of belief in the sanctity of the human person, the only stay against these things.

The neofundamentalists treat the matter as if the central issue were the existence of God or the literal truth of the Bible. They seem to overlook the implications of the dignity conferred on every human being in the narratives of creation. They speak of a right to life, an oddly disembodied phrase which, isolated as it is by them from human context, tends to devalue the incarnate person and is therefore as unbiblical a conception as Bergson's *élan vital.* It invokes Jefferson, but Jefferson posited a divine endowment to every person that includes also liberty and the pursuit of happiness—terms that are difficult to define but that clearly imply dignity and hope and the exercise of meaningful agency. These are rights that, though "inalienable," have to be enabled and respected in society if they are to exist in fact. For example, they more or less require that one come through childhood in a reasonable state of health. Policies that spread and intensify poverty, besides being unbiblical, deprive individuals of what Jefferson called their God-given rights. The thought among anti-Darwinists was, and supposedly still is, that humankind is demeaned by the notion that God was not in every sense present and intentional in the creation of our first parents. The passionate loyalty of the neofundamentalists to the second chapter of Genesis (the first is startlingly compatible with the idea of evolution, though not Darwinism) seems to have prevented them from reading on in the text. Were they to do so, they would find there much to indicate that God continues to be present, and also intentional, in the lives of Eve's children.

Since these folk claim to be defenders of embattled Christianity (under siege by liberalism, as they would have it), they might be struck by the passage in Matthew 25 in which Jesus says, identifying himself with the poorest, "I was hungry, and ye fed me not." This is the parable in which Jesus portrays himself as eschatological judge and in which he separates "the nations." It should surely be noted that he does not apply any standard of creed—of purity or of orthodoxy—in deciding whom to save and whom to damn. This seems to me a valuable insight into what Jesus himself might consider fundamental. To those who have not recognized him in the hungry and the naked, he says, "Depart from me, ye cursed, into the eternal fire which is prepared for the devil and his angels." Neofundamentalists seem to crave this sort of language—more than they might if they were to consider its context here. It is the teaching of the Bible passim that God has confided us very largely to one another's care, but that in doing so he has in no degree detached himself from us. Indeed, in this parable Jesus would seem to push beyond the image of God as final judge to describe an immanence of God in humankind that makes judgment present and continuous, and that in effect makes our victim our judge. Neither here nor anywhere else in the Bible is there the slightest suggestion that our judge/victim would find a plea of economic rationalism extenuating. This supposed new Awakening is to the first two Awakenings, and this neofundamentalism is to the first fundamentalism, as the New Right is to the New Deal, or as matter is to antimatter.

Liberal that I am, I would not presume to doubt the authenticity of the religious experience of anyone at all. Calvinism encourages a robust sense of human fallibility, in particular forbidding the idea that human beings can set any limits to God's grace. I do wish to make very clear that it is a *religious* scruple that causes me to distance myself from the idea of an inhering personal holiness, a holiness realized otherwise than through God's good, and always mysterious, pleasure. I believe in a holiness visited upon any mortal as divinely imputed righteousness, to use the old language, or in the love of the father for his child, to use the old metaphor. The division between the liberals and the "evangelicals" is often treated as falling between the really and the not really religious, the dilettante Christians and those adhering to the true faith. This is the fault of the liberals in large part, because they have neglected their own tradition or have abandoned it in fear that distinctiveness might scuttle ecumenism. Indeed, it is among my hopes in writing this essay to remind those generous spirits of *why* they believe as they do, since they themselves seem to have forgotten. And I hope also to draw a little attention to the fact that the old-time religion is not so old after all, and ought not to be regarded as the Christian faith in a uniquely pure or classic form.

The liberal position on this matter could be seen as a softened predestinarianism. God alone judges, and the hearts of mortals can be known truly only by him, in the light of his grace. It is as true of liberal Protestants now as it was of the old Calvinists that they reject the idea that anyone can achieve salvation by piety or moral rigor or by any other means. After all, Jesus did say, "Not everyone who says to me, 'Lord, Lord,' will enter the kingdom of heaven, but only the one who does the will of my Father in heaven. On that day many will say to me, 'Lord, Lord, did we not prophesy in your name, and cast out demons in your name, and do many deeds of power in your name?' Then I will declare to them, 'I never knew you; go away from me, you evildoers' " (Matthew 7:21–23). And Paul, perhaps alluding to this rather startling teaching of Christ and enlarging on it, said, "If I have prophetic powers, and understand all mysteries and all knowledge, and if I have all faith, so as to remove mountains, but do not have love, I am nothing" (I Corinthians 13:2). Love is crucial here, and not highly compatible with self-interest, even that expressed in heroic self-sacrifice. Ironically, those who have claimed to be defenders of human freedom have tended to set requirements for salvation: being "born again," as they understand the phrase; being baptized at a certain age, under certain conditions, in a particular state of belief; being a member in good standing of a particular church; accepting the authority of a doctrinal system without reference to one's own knowledge or comprehension of it; availing oneself of the salvific benefits that are believed to be at the disposal of a church through its prayers and sacraments. That salvation should be "earned" by any of these means would itself depend on accidents of birth and culture which, being accidents, would only imply predestination in another form. After all, the great mass of human lives have come and gone without access to them. So the justice of God is vindicated, if at all, only locally by these intended empowerments of human beings. What can appear to be empowerments from one side are from another clearly conditions, even coercions. Better, liberally speaking, to trust the free grace of God than to attempt to make oneself proof against an arbitrariness it seems impious to ascribe to him.

Every old argument against predestination can be made against what I have called its softened form. (I intend no disparagement—the major traditions of Christianity are all softened at this point, less preoccupied with damnation than they have been historically and better for the change.) The argument has been made that the insistence on salvation by grace alone would free people to act however they pleased, the assumption being that they would turn to every sort of vice. Lutherans and Calvinists, the traditions among whom this teaching is most emphasized, have never been noted for libertinism, however. In general, their histories suggest that people are pleased to act well when they act freely, at least as often as they act well under any sort of coercion. In present terms, no statistics indicate that any of the vices or pathologies of modern life are more prevalent among liberal Protestants than among any other group.

Predestinarianism has been supposed to result in fatalism, that is, in a stoical passivity relative to the things of this world. But historically Calvinism is strongly associated with social reform as well as with revolution. This might seem a paradox at first glance, but the doctrine had its origins as a forthright teaching (Augustine, Aquinas, and Ignatius of Loyola were also predestinarians) in a context of profound skepticism as to the legitimacy of any number of human institutions and much questioning of their right to claim the Mandate of Heaven. The Reformation was not the work of fatalists. It is still true that liberal Protestants are disproportionately generous and active in support of social justice, a fact that makes them anathema to those who associate Christ with laissez faire economics, as a surprising number of people do these days, absent any endorsement in scripture. Despite their self-proclaimed biblicism, they seem never to miss such endorsement.

There is an asymmetry in the relationship of liberal Protestants to their Christian detractors that is the result of the liberal understanding of the freedom of God. Liberals assume the existence of what is traditionally called "the invisible church." They believe that no institution is uniquely the people of God, that God knows his own whoever they are and wherever they are. And they believe, therefore, that this invisible church can, of course, include their Christian detractors. This view of things implies that no doctrinal tests exist to distinguish the true faith from the false, real Christians from poseurs, the orthodox from the erring. To object, to dispute, to counter text with text, all this is legitimate and necessary, though liberals have been far too hesitant to make their case, even among themselves. But to judge the state of any soul is to presume upon a prerogative God reserves to himself. As Paul says, "Who are you to pass judgment on the servants of another? It is before their own lord that they stand or fall. And they will be upheld, for the Lord is able to make them stand" (Romans 14:4). This is not relativism or lack of conviction. Certainly Paul was never guilty of either. It is deference toward God our Universal Father. And there is nothing easy about suspending judgment. On the contrary, the world is and has been ravaged by the very confident judgments people make of one another. More to the point, history is full of extraordinary acts of ferocity carried out by Christians against Christians. Self-styled defenders of the faith have left the faith sorely wounded, in its good name not least.

There is a Hebrew root transliterated as *ndb* that is rendered in English by such words as free, noble, generous, abundant, and liberal and their forms. It is used of God and of virtuous human beings and behaviors. It occurs in Isaiah 32:5, a messianic context. In the 1611 King James Version, it is rendered thus:

> The instruments also of the churle are evill: he deviseth wicked devices, to destroy the poore with lying wordes even when the needie speaketh right. But the liberall deviseth liberall things, and by liberall things shall hee stand.

More modern translations render the word as "noble," which clarifies its meaning. In Deuteronomy 15:14 the same principle of nobility is applied in reference to the treatment of the poor. "When you send a male slave out from you a free person, you shall not send him out empty-handed. Provide liberally out of your flock, your threshing floor, and your wine press, thus giving to him some of the bounty with which the Lord your God has blessed you."

Ndb—let us call it "liberality"—occurs in a context that continually reinforces an ethic of liberality, that is, the Old Testament. The many economic laws God gives to Israel as a society are full of provisions for the widow and the orphan, the poor and the stranger. And the abuses the prophets decry most passionately are accumulations of wealth in contempt of these same laws.

And as for Jesus: A ruler asks him how he is to inherit eternal life, and Jesus replies, "Sell all that you own and distribute the money to the poor" (Luke 18:22). How on earth his teaching is to be reconciled with social conservatism I cannot imagine, though the question seems seldom to be asked. (I use the phrase "social conservatism," which might seem to imply moral conservatism, unless, like God, one considers generosity an essential part of morality.) There is a powerful contemporary Christianism that admires Dives and emulates him and regards Lazarus as burdensome and reprehensible. Indeed, the supposed Christian revival of the present moment has given something very like unlimited moral authority to money, though Jesus did say (and I think a literal interpretation is appropriate here if anywhere) "Woe to you who are rich!" (Luke 6:24). If this seems radical, dangerous, unfair, un-American, then those who make such criticisms should at least have the candor to acknowledge that their quarrel is with Jesus.

We all err, of course. We all come short of the glory of God, as Paul taught us. And as Christian liberalism teaches us as well. Calvin wrote about "total depravity," which has a terrible sound because of the modern meaning of a word that, when he used it (that is, in the French and Latin it derives from) meant warped or distorted. He was rejecting the teaching of Catholic theology that baptism erased the consequences of the Fall from the higher functions, so that only the lower functions, particularly sexuality, continued to be affected by it. No, there is always error in all our thinking and perceiving, according to Calvin. Or as Paul said, speaking to Christians as a Christian, "We see in a glass, darkly." This acknowledgment of the fact of inescapable fallibility has been called the origin of scientific method, and in this form we know that doubt and self-doubt are allied with truth—teaching as they do that truth as we can know it remains forever partial and provisional.

This doctrine is very liberal in its consequences, an excellent basis for the harmony in diversity that is an essential liberal value and that is now under attack as relativism or as an unprincipled concession to what is now called secularism. This secularism, which is supposed to alarm us, in fact may be nothing more alien to religion than the common space our many flourishing religious traditions have long been accustomed to share. In any case, it is worth remembering that such a common, nonjudgmental space is fully consistent with faithful doubt, as it were, which has not only the very humane consequence of allowing us to live together in peace and mutual respect, but also a strong theological and scriptural grounding. It is first of all the responsibility of liberal or mainline Protestantism to remember this, because insofar as it is an aspect of their tradition, they should understand it and be able to speak for it. A very great deal depends on its being understood and defended.

I may seem to have wandered from my original subject. What has personal holiness to do with politics and economics? Everything, from the liberal Protestant point of view. They are the means by which our poor and orphaned and our strangers can be sustained in real freedom, and graciously, as God requires. How can a Christian live without certainty? More fully, I suspect, than one can live with doctrines that constrict the sense of God with definitions and conditions.

It is vision that floods the soul with the sense of holiness, vision of this world. And it is reverent attention to this world that teaches us, and teaches us again, the imperatives of ethical refinement.

"We ought to embrace the whole human race without exception in a single feeling of love; here there is no distinction between barbarian and Greek, worthy and unworthy, friend and enemy, since all should be contemplated in God, not in themselves. When we turn aside from such contemplation, it is no wonder we become entangled in many errors." This is John Calvin, describing in two sentences a mystical/ethical engagement with the world that fuses truth and love and that opens experience on a light so bright it expunges every mean distinction. There is no doctrine here, no conditions, no drawing of lines. On the contrary, what he describes is a posture of grace, generosity, liberality.

The People of the (Unread) Book

BILL McKIBBEN

Go and learn what this means: "I desire mercy, not sacrifice."
—*Matthew* 9:13

Only 40 percent of Americans can name more than five of the Ten Commandments, and a scant half can cite any of the four authors of the gospels. Twelve percent believe Joan of Arc was Noah's wife. This failure to recall the specifics of our Judeo-Christian heritage may be further evidence of our nation's educational decline, but it probably doesn't matter all that much in spiritual or political terms. Here is a statistic that does matter: Three-quarters of Americans believe that the Bible says "God helps those who help themselves." That is, three out of four Americans believe that this uber-American idea, a notion at the core of our current individualist politics and culture, which was in fact uttered by Ben Franklin, actually appears in holy scripture. The thing is, not only is Franklin's wisdom not biblical, it's *counter*-biblical. Few ideas could be farther from the gospel message, with its radical summons to love of neighbor. On this essential matter, most Americans—most American *Christians*—are simply wrong, as if 75 percent of American scientists believed that Newton proved gravity causes apples to fly up.

Asking a Christian what Christ taught isn't a trick. When we say we are a Christian nation—and, overwhelmingly, we do—it means something. People who go to church absorb lessons there and make real decisions based on those lessons; increasingly, it informs their politics. (One poll found that 11 percent of U.S. churchgoers had been urged by their clergy to vote in a particular way in 2004, up from 6 percent in 2000.) When George Bush says that Jesus Christ is his favorite philosopher, he may or may not be sincere, but he is reflecting the sincere beliefs of the vast majority of Americans.

And therein is the paradox. America is simultaneously the most professedly Christian of the developed nations and the least Christian in its behavior. That paradox—more important, perhaps, than the much-touted ability of French women to stay thin on a diet of chocolate and cheese—illuminates the hollow at the core of our boastful, careening culture.

America is probably the most spiritually homogenous rich nation on earth. Depending on which poll you look at and how the question is asked, somewhere between 80 and 88 percent of us call ourselves Christian. Israel, by way of comparison, is 77 percent Jewish. It is true that a significantly smaller number of Americans—about 60 percent—claim they actually pray to God on a daily basis, and only 40 percent say they manage to get to church every week. Still, even if that 80 percent overstates actual practice, it clearly represents aspiration. In fact, there is nothing else that unites four-fifths of Americans. Every other statistic one can cite about American behavior is essentially also a measure of the behavior of professed Christians. That's what America is: a place saturated in Christian identity.

But is it *Christian?* This is not a matter of angels dancing on the heads of pins. Christ was pretty specific about what he had in mind for his followers. What if we chose some simple criterion—say, giving aid to the poorest people—as a reasonable proxy for Christian behavior? After all, in the days before his Crucifixion, when Jesus summed up his message for his disciples, he said the way you could tell the righteous from the damned was by whether they'd fed the hungry, slaked the thirsty, clothed the naked, welcomed the stranger, and visited the prisoner. What would we find then?

In 2003, as a share of our economy, we ranked dead last among developed countries in government foreign aid. Per capita we each provided 15¢ a day in official development assistance to poor countries. And that's not because we were giving to private charities for relief work instead—such funding increased our average daily donation by just six pennies, to 21¢. It's also not because Americans were too busy taking care of their own—22 percent of American children lived in poverty (compared with, say, 3 percent in Sweden). In fact, by pretty much any measure of caring for the least among us—childhood nutrition, infant mortality, access to preschool—we come in last among the rich nations, and often by a wide margin. The point is not just that (as everyone already knows) the American nation trails badly in all these categories, it's that the overwhelmingly *Christian* American nation trails badly in all these categories—categories to which Jesus paid particular attention. And it's not as if the numbers are getting better: the USDA reported in 2004 that the percentage of households in which there was hunger due to poverty had climbed 22 percent since 1999.

This Christian nation also tends to make personal, as opposed to political, choices that the Bible would seem to frown upon. Despite the sixth commandment, we are, of course, the most violent rich nation on earth, with a murder rate four or five times that of our European peers. We have prison populations greater by a factor of four or five than other rich nations (which at least should give us plenty of opportunity for visiting). Having been told to turn the other cheek, we're the only rich nation left that executes its citizens, mostly in those states where Christianity is theoretically strongest. Despite Jesus's strong declarations against divorce, our marriages break up at a rate—4.95 per 1,000 people—that compares poorly with the European average of 1.6 per 1,000. That average may be held down by the fact that Europeans marry less frequently and by countries like Italy, where divorce is difficult; still, compare our success with, say, godless Finland, where the divorce rate is 1.85 per 1,000. Teenage pregnancy? We're at the top of the charts. Personal self-discipline—like, say, keeping your weight under control? Buying on credit? Running government deficits? Do you need to ask?[1]

Are Americans hypocrites? Of course they are. But most people (me, for instance) are hypocrites. The more troubling explanation for this disconnect between belief and action, I think, is that most Americans—which means most believers—have replaced the Christianity of the Bible, with its call for deep sharing and personal sacrifice, with a competing creed.

In fact there may be several competing creeds. For many Christians, deciphering a few passages of the Bible to figure out the schedule for the end-time has become a central task. You can log on to RaptureReady .com for a taste of how some of these believers view the world—at this writing the Rapture Index had declined three points to 152 because, despite an increase in the number of U.S. pagans, "Wal-Mart is falling behind in its plan to bar code all products with radio tags." Other end-timers are more interested in forcing the issue—they are convinced that the way to coax the Lord back to earth is to "Christianize" our nation and then the world. Consider House GOP leader Tom DeLay. At church one day he listened as his pastor, urging his flock to support the administration, declared that "the war between America and Iraq is the gateway to the Apocalypse." DeLay rose to speak, not only to the congregation but to 225 Christian TV and radio stations. "Ladies and gentlemen, " he said, "what has been spoken here tonight is the truth of God."

The apocalyptics may not be wrong. One could make a perfectly serious argument that the policies of people like DeLay are in fact hastening the end-time. But there is nothing particularly Christian about this hastening. The creed of Tom DeLay and his pastor—of Tim LaHaye and his *Left Behind* books, of Pat Roberston's "The Antichrist is probably a Jew alive in Israel today"—ripened out of the impossibly poetic imagery of the book of Revelation. Imagine trying to build a theory of the Constitution by obsessively reading and rereading the Twenty-fifth Amendment, and you'll get an idea of what an odd approach this is. You might be able to spin elaborate fantasies about presidential succession, but you would have a hard time working backward to "We the People." This is the contemporary version of Archbishop Ussher's seventeenth-century calculation that the world had been created on October 23, 4004 BC, and that Noah's Ark touched down on Mount Ararat on May 5, 2348 BC, a Wednesday. Interesting, but a distant distraction from the gospel message. This stuff is *in* the Bible (cryptically), but it's not what the Bible is *about*.

But the apocalyptics are the lesser problem. It is another competing (though sometimes overlapping) creed, this one straight from the sprawling megachurches of the new exurbs, that frightens me most. Its deviation is less obvious precisely because it looks so much like the rest of the culture. In fact, most of what gets preached in these palaces isn't loony at all. It is disturbingly conventional. The pastors focus relentlessly on *you* and on your individual needs. Their goal is to service consumers. Not communities but individuals: "seekers" is the term of art, people who feel the need for some spirituality in their (or their children's) lives, but who are not tightly bound to any particular denomination or school of thought. The result is often a kind of soft-focus, comfortable suburban faith.

A *New York Times* reporter visiting one booming megachurch outside Phoenix recently found the typical scene: a drive-through latte stand, Krispy Kreme donuts at every service, and sermons about "how to discipline your children, how to reach your professional goals, how to invest your money, how to reduce your debt." On Sundays, children played with church-distributed Xboxes, and many congregants had signed up for a twice-weekly aerobics class called Firm Believers. A list of best sellers compiled monthly by the Christian Booksellers Association illuminates the creed. It includes texts like *Your Best Life Now*—by Joel Osteen, pastor of a church so mega it recently bought a sixteen-thousand-seat basketball arena in Houston for its services—which even the normally tolerant religion editor of *Publishers Weekly* dismissed as "a treatise on how to get God to serve the demands of self-centered individuals." Nearly as high on the list is Beth Moore, with her *Believing God*—"Beth asks the tough questions concerning the fruit of our Christian lives: are we living as fully as we can?" Other titles include *Humor for a Woman's Heart,* a collection of "humorous writings" designed to "lift a life above the stresses and strains of the day"; *Five Love Languages,* in which Dr. Gary Chapman helps you figure out if you're speaking in the same emotional dialect as your significant other; and Karol Ladd's *The Power of a Positive Woman.* Ladd is the founder of USA Sonshine Girls—the "Son" in sonshine, of course, is the Son of God—and she is unremittingly upbeat in presenting her five-part plan for creating a life with "more calm and less stress."

Not that any of this is so bad in itself. We *do* have stressful lives, humor *does* help, and you *should* pay attention to your own needs. Comfortable suburbanites watch their parents die, their kids implode. Clearly I need help with being positive. And I have no doubt that such texts have turned people into better parents, better spouses, better bosses. It's just that these authors, in presenting their perfectly sensible advice, somehow manage to ignore Jesus's radical and demanding focus on *others*. That is, it may in fact be true that "God helps those who help themselves," both financially and emotionally. (Certainly fortune does.) But if so, it is still a subsidiary, secondary truth, more Franklinity than Christianity. You could eliminate the scriptural references in most of these best sellers and they would still make or not make the same amount of sense. *Chicken Soup for the Zoroastrian Soul.* It is a perfect mirror of the secular best-seller lists, and indeed of the secular culture, with its American fixation on self-improvement, on self-esteem. On self. These similarities make it difficult (although clearly not impossible) for the televangelists to posit themselves as embattled figures in a "culture war"—they offer too uncanny a reflection of the dominant culture, a culture of unrelenting self-obsession.

Who am I to criticize someone else's religion? After all, if there is anything Americans agree on it's that we should tolerate everyone else's religious expression. As a *Newsweek* writer put it some years ago at the end of his cover story on apocalyptic visions and the book of Revelation, "Who's to say that John's mythic battle between Christ and Antichrist is not a valid insight into what the history of humankind is all about?" (Not *Newsweek*, that's for sure; their religious covers are guaranteed big sellers). To that I can only answer that I'm a . . . Christian.

Not a professional one; I'm an environmental writer mostly. I've never progressed farther in the church hierarchy than Sunday school teacher at my backwoods Methodist church. But I've spent most of my Sunday mornings in a pew. I grew up in church youth groups and stayed active most of my adult life—started homeless shelters in church basements, served soup at the church food pantry, climbed to the top of the rickety ladder to put the star on the church Christmas tree. I've been a seminary trustee, a guest preacher, and the guy who changed the storm windows in the sanctuary every fall and spring. My work has been, at times, influenced by all that—I've written extensively about the book of Job, which is to me the first great piece of nature writing in the Western tradition, and about the overlaps between Christianity and environmentalism. In fact, I imagine I am one of a fairly small number of writers who have had cover stories in both the *Christian Century*, the magazine of liberal mainline Protestantism, and *Christianity Today*, which Billy Graham founded, not to mention articles in *Sojourners*, the magazine of the progressive evangelical community founded by Jim Wallis.

Indeed, it was my work with religious environmentalists that first got me thinking along the lines of this essay. We were trying to get politicians to understand why the Bible actually mandated protecting the world around us (Noah: the first Green), work that I think is true and vital. Sometimes I'd say to people that religious institutions were the only institutions left in our society that could posit some reason for existence other than accumulation, and hence they were key potential allies in the environmental fight. But one day it occurred to me that the parts of the world where people actually *had* cut dramatically back on their carbon emissions, actually *did* live voluntarily in smaller homes and take public transit, were the same countries where people were giving aid to the poor and making sure everyone had health care—countries like Denmark and Norway and Sweden, where religion is relatively unimportant. How could that be? Maybe it had to do with Scandinavia's Christian heritage—Danish king Harald Bluetooth converted in AD 960, giving his progeny a millennium to absorb the faith, even if lately they've lapsed. Or maybe it was something else entirely—reason, or scientific literacy, or eating smoked salmon. For Christians there should be something at least a little scary in the notion that, absent the magical answers of religion, people might just get around to solving their problems and strengthening their communities in more straightforward ways.

But for me, in any event, the European success is less interesting than the American failure. Because we're not going to be like them. Maybe we would be better off if we abandoned religion for secular rationality, but we're not going to; for the foreseeable future this will be a "Christian" nation. The question is, what *kind* of Christian nation?

The tendencies I've been describing—toward an apocalyptic end-time faith, toward a comfort-the-comfortable personal empowerment faith—veil the actual, and remarkable, message of the gospels. When one of the Pharisees asked Jesus what the core of the law was, Jesus replied:

> Thou shalt love the Lord thy God with all they heart, and with all thy soul, and with all thy mind. This is the first and great commandment. And the second is like unto it, Thou shalt love thy neighbor as thyself. On these two commandments hang all the law and the prophets.

Love thy neighbor as thyself—though its rhetorical power has been dimmed by repetition, that is a radical notion, perhaps the most radical notion possible. Especially since Jesus, in all his teachings, made it very clear who the neighbor you were supposed to love was: the poor person, the sick person, the naked person, the hungry person. The last shall be made first; turn the other cheek; a rich person aiming for heaven is like a camel trying to walk through the eye of a needle. On and on and on—a call for nothing less than a radical, voluntary, and effective reordering of power relationships, based on the principle of love.

I confess, even as I write these words, to a feeling close to embarrassment. Because in public we tend not to talk about such things—my theory of what Jesus mostly meant seems like it should be left in church, or confined to some religious publication. But remember the overwhelming connection between America and Christianity: what Jesus meant is the most deeply potent political, cultural, social question. To ignore it, or leave it to the bullies and the salesmen of the televangelist sects, means to walk away from a central battle over American identity. At the moment, the idea of Jesus has been hijacked by people with a series of causes that do not reflect his teachings. The Bible is a long book, and even the gospels have plenty in them, some of it seemingly contradictory and hard to puzzle out. But love your neighbor as yourself—not do unto others as you would have them do unto you, but *love your neighbor as yourself*—will suffice as a gloss. There is no disputing the centrality of this message, nor is there any disputing how easy it is to ignore that message. Because it is so counterintuitive, Christians have had to keep repeating it to themselves right from the start. Consider Paul, for instance, writing to the church at Galatea: "All the law is fulfilled in one word," he said, "even in this: 'You shall love your neighbor as yourself.'"

American churches, by and large, have done a pretty good job of loving the neighbor in the next pew. A pastor can spend all Sunday talking about the Rapture Index, but if his congregation is thriving you can be assured he's spending the other six days visiting people in the hospital, counseling couples, and sitting up with grieving widows. All this human connection is important. But if the theology makes it harder to love the neighbor a little further away—particularly the poor and the weak—then it's a problem. And the dominant theologies of the moment do just that. They undercut Jesus, muffle his hard words, deaden his call, in the end silence him. In fact, the soft-focus consumer gospel of the suburban megachurches is a perfect match for emergent conservative economic notions about personal responsibility instead of collective action. Privatize Social Security? Keep health care for people who can afford it? File those under "God helps those who help themselves."

Take Alabama as an example. In 2002 Bob Riley was elected governor of the state, where more than 90 percent of residents identify themselves as Christians. Riley could safely be called a conservative—right-wing majordomo Grover Norquist had given him a Friend of the Taxpayer Award every year he was in Congress, where he'd never voted for a tax increase. But when he took over Alabama, he found himself administering a tax code that dated to 1901. The richest Alabamians paid 3 percent of their income in taxes, and the poorest paid 12 percent; income taxes kicked in if a family of four made $4,600 (even in Mississippi the threshold was $19,000), while out-of-state timber companies paid

$1.25 an acre in property taxes. Alabama was fiftieth in total state and local taxes; what revenue it did raise tended to come from sales tax—a superregressive tax that in some counties reached into double digits. So Riley proposed a property tax increase, the largest in the state's history, partly to dig the state out of a fiscal crisis and partly to put more money into the state's school system, routinely ranked worst in the nation. He argued that it was Christian duty to look after the poor more carefully.

Had the new law passed, the owner of a $250,000 home would have paid $1,540 in property taxes—we're not talking Sweden here. But it didn't pass. It was crushed by a factor of two to one. Sixty-eight percent of the state voted against it—meaning, of course, something like 68 percent of the Christians who voted. The opposition was led, in fact, not just by the state's wealthiest interests but also by the Alabama Christian Coalition. "You'll find most Alabamians have got a charitable heart," said John Giles, the group's president, as reported in the *New York Times*. "They just don't want it coming out of their pockets." On its Web site, the group argued that taxing the rich at a higher rate than the poor "results in punishing success. . . . *We believe that when an individual works for their income, that money belongs to the individual*." You might as well just cite chapter and verse from *Poor Richard's Almanack*. And whatever the ideology, the results are clear. "We are first in everything bad," said Governor Riley, "and last in everything good."

A rich young man came to Jesus one day and asked what he should do to live a more godly life. Jesus did not say he should invest, spend, and let the benefits trickle down; he said, "Sell what you have, give the money to the poor, and follow me." Few plainer words have been spoken. And yet, for some reason, the Christian Coalition of America—founded in 1989, according to its Web site, in order to "preserve, protect and defend the Judeo-Christian values that made this the greatest country in history"—proclaimed in 2004 that its top legislative priority would be "making permanent President Bush's 2001 federal tax cuts."

Similarly, a furor erupted when it emerged that a Colorado jury had consulted the Bible before sentencing a killer to death. The legal controversy the papers covered centered on whether the (Christian) jurors should have used an "outside authority" in their deliberations, and of course the Christian Right saw it as one more sign of a secular society devaluing religion. But a more interesting question would have been why the jurors fixated on Leviticus 24, with its call for "an eye for an eye and a tooth for a tooth." They had somehow missed Jesus's explicit refutation in the New Testament: "You have heard that it was said, 'an eye for an eye and a tooth for a tooth.' But I tell you, don't resist him who is evil, but whoever strikes you on your right cheek, turn to him the other also."

And on and on. The power of the Christian Right rests largely in the fact that they boldly claim religious authority, and by their very boldness convince the rest of us that they must know what they're talking about. They're like the guy who gives you directions with such loud confidence that you follow them even though the road appears to be turning into a faint, rutted track. But their theology is appealing for another reason, too: it coincides with what we want to believe. The gospel is too radical for any culture larger than the Amish to ever come close to realizing; in demanding a departure from selfishness it conflicts with all our current desires. How nice it would be if Jesus *had* declared that our income was ours to keep, instead of insisting, in as many ways as he could think of to say it, that we had to share. How satisfying it would be if we were *supposed* to hate our enemies. Religious conservatives will always have a comparatively easy sell.

"Straight is the path and narrow is the way." If there is one thing Christians should be suspicious of, it's a creed that serves their own superficial ends: The gospels were good news to the poor, but—judging by the reaction—they were pretty unwelcome news to an awful lot of other people. So there is not going to be a modern-day return to the church of the early believers, holding all things in common—that's not what I'm talking about. But taking seriously the actual message of Jesus should serve at least to moderate the greed and violence that mark this culture. It's hard to imagine a con much more audacious than making Christ the front man for a program of tax cuts for the rich or war in Iraq. If some modest part of the 85 percent of us who are Christians woke up to that fact, then the world might change.

It is possible, I think. Yes, the mainline Protestant churches that were instrumental in supporting civil rights and opposing the war in Vietnam are mostly locked in a dreary decline as their congregations dwindle and their elders argue endlessly about gay clergy and same-sex unions. And the Catholic Church, for most of its American history a sturdy exponent of a "love your neighbor" theology, has been weakened too, its hierarchy increasingly motivated by a single-issue focus on abortion. I am well aware that there are plenty of vital congregations and parishes doing great good works—they're the ones that have nurtured me. But they aren't precisely where the challenge will come from, in part because they've grown shy about talking about Jesus, more comfortable with the language of sociology and politics. More and more it's Bible-quoting Christians, like Wallis's Sojourners movement, who are carrying the fight. Because their appeal is rooted in the plain words of the gospels, it can reach deep inside those cultures that too many dismiss as ignorant. Not ignorant, just misled.

And these cultures have one virtue: when they recognize something as a truth they often actually act on it. The best selling of all evangelical books in recent years, Rick Warren's *The Purpose-Driven Life,* illustrates the possibilities. It has all the hallmarks of self-absorption (in one five-page chapter I counted eighty-five uses of the word *you*), but it also makes a powerful case that we're made for mission. What that mission *is* never becomes completely clear, but the thirst for it is real. And there's no great need for Warren to state that purpose anyhow. For Christians, the plainspoken message of the gospels is clear enough. If you have any doubts, read the Sermon on the Mount. That would be in Matthew, starting with the fifth chapter.

Admittedly, this is hope against hope; more likely the money changers and power brokers will remain ascendant in our "spiritual" life. Since the days of Constantine, emperors and rich men have sought to co-opt the teachings of Jesus. As in so many other areas of our increasingly market-tested lives, the co-opters—the TV men, the politicians, the Christian "interest groups"—have now found a way to make every one of us complicit in that travesty as well. They have invited us to subvert the church of Jesus even as we celebrate it. With their help, we have made golden calves of ourselves—become a nation of terrified, self-obsessed idols. I-dolaters. It works, and it may well keep working for a long time to come. When Americans hunger for selfless love and are fed only love of self, they will remain hungry.

Note

1. One possible explanation for these anomalies that was much discussed after last fall's presidential election is that the American heartland, suffused in real Christian values, is surrounded by an arc of value-deficient liberal states that somehow throw off the curve. However, the vast majority of Americans in every single state consider themselves Christian. Indeed, by some measures, Rhode Island has the highest rate of religious affiliation in America. In any case, the Kerry-voting states hewed to Christian teachings as much as the Bush-voting states, even by conservative standards. Abortion rates are lower across the Bible Belt, for instance, but divorce rates are consistently 50 percent higher than in the rest of the country.

Higher Ground: The Nonviolence Imperative

JAMES M. LAWSON, JR.

Love your enemies, and pray for those who persecute you, so that you may be children of your Father in heaven.

—*Matthew* 5:44–45

I woke up this morning with my mind stayed on Jesus.

I did not expect this to happen. I did not plan for this to happen. I really had little to do with making it happen. I cannot say *when* this happened: I cannot name a day or time or season.

Nevertheless, one morning I became aware of this startling and amazing thing: there was no animosity or fear or envy in my heart toward those who did not want me to be. I did not hate those who had sought to harm me. There was not the slightest wish to injure the white people who harbored racial animosity toward me. Instead, I felt a profound sense of well-being before God. I knew that my life was truly meant to be. I felt a profound awareness that God's love leaves no space for despising anyone, certainly not for despising the people this nation and this society urged me to despise.

Jesus had taught me to love my enemies and love those who would mistreat and abuse me. In the same movement of the spirit I found the resources to allow my heart to sing the music of compassion. I knew myself to be a beloved child of God in a society that certainly did not love me, and that desperately sought to diminish me or even extinguish me through the force of its racism.

I now think I know a little more about this and about its relevance for all Christians. But first I must describe the context of my discovery.

In the winter of 1932 my father, Rev. James M. Lawson, Sr., was appointed pastor of the St. James AME Zion Church in Massillon, Ohio.

Ten of us drove there from a town in Pennsylvania, where Dad had completed his previous charge. Our two cars followed the moving van. My consciousness was etched by what happened next, when we reached our new house. Dad brought a large chair from the van and placed it in our new dining room. He told me to sit. He went out and in a few moments returned, carrying my baby brother, Philip. He placed Philip on my lap and showed me how to hold him. I was to care for the infant while all of the others moved us into that new home.

It was on Tremont Street in Massillon that I was first called "nigger." I was just four. From the very first I struck out against such assaults with my fists and my whole body. We Lawson children could not accept any such treatment. This was the kind of hate-filled language *we* were not allowed to use. Both of my parents stressed the love of God and our essential humanity, but they had differing views of what nonacceptance of others' contempt should mean—and even of what an appropriate response to another's incidental anger should mean.

My mother insisted that even when one of us was upset, we were still to speak to each other with gentle language: that is, we were to treat each other as we would want to be treated. Dad's philosophy was the same, but his practical counsel was different. I recall an occasion when my brother Bill and I became very angry with each other. Dad told us to go outside and fight it out. Mom firmly protested, "Now, Jacob . . ."

I recall one encounter with a white boy who stood about ten inches taller than me. I was eight or nine years old. Without hesitation I rushed at him with my fists, saying not a word. We fought and wrestled for several minutes and wore each other out, giving each other bruises and bloody noses. We yelled and we grunted, but still no words were exchanged. We walked away silently, exhausted. But he was still not my "enemy." Even though by that time the twenty-third Psalm had entered my consciousness, thanks to our family devotions, I had not yet absorbed the meaning of enemy or connected the concept of enemy with my own repeated experiences of racism.

At this age I was deeply into football, cycling, softball, running, stone-throwing "wars," and wrestling with my younger brothers. When I started the first grade at a school located eight blocks up the hill from our house, getting to school meant passing under a railroad viaduct and passing over the Tuscarawas River Bridge. Here the larger neighborhood came together, and here I had to submit to the "preacher's kid" gantlet. For months boy after boy, egged on by our classmates, taunted and pressed me until we fought. So far as I remember, I won each of these fights. This pattern culminated with the neighborhood boys matching me against the one boy in a higher grade whom they considered certain to beat me.

I do not know why I resisted every prompting to get me to fight. I arrived home that day marching up the steps and making the kind of racket that signals a state of high commotion. As I crossed through the living room my father asked me what was going on. I told him. He told me to go out and fight that boy. I no longer hesitated; the next day I spent the lunch hour fighting the older, bigger, and heavier boy. But the eggers-on were disappointed because I was not beaten, despite the headache I carried away. The eggers-on were themselves beaten by the realization that they now needed to get back to class or risk a penalty for tardiness.

This was my last true gladiatorial bout. For years afterward, I enjoyed boxing and various other physical education pursuits, but viewing my fists as a necessary and even valorous element of life had been overthrown in me.

It was a resplendent spring day in 1937 or 1938. My parents had purchased a lovely property on Groose Avenue some ten blocks to the south of Tremont Street. Three of my brothers and I then attended Horace Mann School just four blocks from our back-yard. On this day I raced home when my last class ended, came in through the back door and into the kitchen to greet my mother. She asked me to run an errand for her and gave me instructions. I headed off to Main Street, which was six blocks away. Just as I got to Main and turned left into a row of small retail shops, I walked past a parked car that had its windows rolled down. In that car sat a young white kid who easily snaked his entire head and shoulders out of the car to yell "Nigger!" at me at the top of his voice. Just as easily, I walked over to the car, calmly but soundly slapped this boy's face, and just as calmly moved on to complete my errand.

On making my purchase and returning along the way I had come, I noticed that the car was gone. Back in my mother's kitchen and seated in a favorite spot just to the right of the back door, I did not at first relate to her the slapping incident on Main Street. When I did mention it, Mother and I just continued to talk, she with her voice unruffled and her back turned to me as she continued to work over the big range in that kitchen. Yet in that warm and peaceful place my world and my life came to a standstill—a standstill sheathed in indescribable silence. For me the entire house went silent.

I can still picture my mother at that stove. There were at least nine people in the house. Often we were noisy and full of talk and laughter and play. We sang a lot. My four brothers and I were always into something. The members of my family were musicians and we all listened to the radio. Yet no evidence of this boisterous household life was present to me then. Just that stillness and within it my mother's loving voice.

I still hear her first sentence: "*Jim*mie," she said, with an emphasis to make me sure to pay attention, "what good did that do?"

I cannot recall many of her other words, except that she rehearsed with me our core family values: God, love for one another, life in the church, and most of all what we had learned from Jesus. My mother insisted then on telling me who I was and on telling me that no mean words could ever take away my status before God and before my family. "I love you," she said. "We love you." I cannot perfectly recall how all of this ended, except for Mother's very last sentence: "Jimmie, there must be a better way!"

As she says this I remain in a bubble of silence apart from her voice. Somewhere I hear another voice that I do not recognize. It seems to come from beyond the silence, beyond my mother or myself. It sounds from beyond that time and space. And it is certainly not my voice, even though in comes from out of the depths of me. It is not my voice, yet I also hear that it *is* my voice. I hear two things. The first is that I will never again fight on the street. The second is that I will find a better way.

The moment was decisive; it launched my lifelong search for the better way. Encounters with the fears and racism of white people continued to be a constant. I had no shortage of opportunities to shove or to swing my fists on the playing fields. But never again did I launch a fight in retaliation for an injury—not on the streets or in the parks or on the football field. Instead I used my head and heart, my voice and my wit, to turn the other cheek. In the process I discovered that my anger could turn into the energy I needed to play harder and better.

In high school I intensified my study of the four gospels and Jesus. The Sermon on the Mount became my spiritual North Star. In college at Baldwin Wallace I began formally to read Gandhi, recognizing that Gandhi offered me a language that resonated with the spirit of Jesus. In learning to live out of love, as I understood my mother's admonition to me, I continued also to develop my ability to resist evil. When met with hostility on campus I often turned to my assailant so as to place myself gently up against his or her prejudice. I would often see people's hostility melt away.

My awakening continued when Rev. A. J. Muste, renowned leader of the Fellowship of Reconciliation (FOR), spoke at my college. Hearing about Christian pacifism made me aware that my own search was not a solitary one. Muste also applied the mind of Jesus to the world scene and to a critique of World War II, which I had strongly supported up until that point. Through the FOR I learned of James Farmer, George Hauser, and Bayard Rustin, who were already using nonviolence to break down racial discrimination. I learned from their work. I participated in my first sit-in at the Sugar Bowl restaurant in Massillon during Christmas break in 1947. The management did not budge. A white student and I went to a local diner together. Refused again. There were many such episodes.

In those early college years, I discovered that I did not hate or fear the enemy. But I resisted the enmity, because now I was learning also how white racism had constructed a fierce enmity against me simply because of the color of my skin—a gift of creation. In those years I began to take the measure of the oppression forged and forced upon black people and other people of color. I refused to run or hide. I sought simply to follow Jesus and to learn how to resist. I considered Jesus to be an extraordinary pragmatist. He knew that "an eye for an eye," enmity for enmity, hatred for hatred, slap for slap, exalted the wrong and undermined the right. He knew that one can sabotage one's own gift of life by imitating the evil one experiences. Instead of imitating evil, I tried to imitate Jesus.

Yes, I woke up one morning with my mind stayed on Jesus. And on love and beauty and truth—on nonviolent struggle—on the community of support and of justice. This arrived as an unexpected gift, rooted in an unconditional and unconventional love.

I now discovered in Christ's gospel a life-shattering power; I discovered in the teachings of Jesus the better way to resist prejudice and racism. And through the Fellowship of Reconciliation I also discovered Dr. Howard Thurman, a pastor who served as a national officer in the FOR. In 1949 Thurman authored a most remarkable book—*Jesus and the Disinherited*—in which he wrote: "The basic fact is that Christianity as it was born in the mind of this Jewish teacher and thinker appears as a technique of survival for the oppressed." This powerfully affirmed my own experiences.

Christians in our country are quite willing to proclaim Jesus as Lord and Savior. American Christians do not, however, claim the spirit, the mind, the heart, and the soul of Jesus as the content of how they are to live. This is understandable. The thought and spirituality of Jesus is even more radical and revolutionary in today's context than it was in the first century. Our dogma about Jesus the Savior prevents us from following Jesus the Jew, Jesus the prophet, Jesus the healer, Jesus the preacher, Jesus the teacher, Jesus the resurrecter of human lives, Jesus the good news for *all* of life, Jesus the carpenter who repairs our life houses, Jesus the word of God in flesh and blood, Jesus the lover of life, Jesus the authentic revolutionary, Jesus the spiritual director, and Jesus the glory of God: that is, Jesus who shows the whole world how God's glory is accessible to *any* ordinary woman or man.

The visible practice of Christianity in this land does not reflect what Jesus taught or how he thought or lived. It reflects instead an un-Christian ultranationalism that is saturated with white racism. Such public Christianity is thus an unholy amalgam, openly contemptuous of the poor and marginalized. But Jesus walked and talked all over his land of first-century Palestine, showing forth the light and love of God in the midst of life and all its messiness. Jesus dramatized the good news of God's love for all by going out to the people, by feeding the hungry, by healing the demon-ridden and the diseased, by calling men and women alike to the work of the kingdom, by referring to little children as signs of God, by welcoming sinners and bringing the ostracized into the community, by confronting hypocritical religionists while drawing the real spiritual searchers to his side, by overthrowing the tables of corruption, by overcoming evil with good, and by insisting that God invites all people to the feast.

The four gospel accounts *show us* what Jesus did; they describe him moving through the territory, marching from crossroads to village to city. It is crystal clear that he was seriously disrupting daily life—causing public disturbances—in Galilee and Judea and Samaria. Do you suppose for one minute that the authorities were blind or unaware of this? Think about what Jesus was doing and then study the church-grounded movements that formed the heart of the modern Black Freedom Movement, a movement symbolized by the names of Rosa Parks and Martin King. I was engaged in those struggles myself, while still reading the gospels every day and preaching to my congregation almost every Sunday. Little did *I* know at that time whose pattern or modus operandi we were unconsciously living out.

Jesus became the flowering zenith of the prophetic spirituality flowing from his own Jewish tradition. Matthew 5:38–48 supplies the summation of his theological and spiritual genius. While we find clues and hints of these insights within the Hebrew Bible and in other fist-century writings, no one before Jesus presented the message in quite this way. The fact that this message arises unmistakably from the center of Judaism makes the protracted conflict between what became a Gentile-led movement and its Jewish parent a tragic misdirection in religious history. For its part, the early Jesus movement soon tried to shear Jesus of his prophetic roots; it also allowed the "Christ killer" libel against the Jews to flourish. Faced with this, Judaism was forced not only to reject Jesus as God's anointed but also to reject him as an authentic Jew and a remarkable prophet. Tragic misdirection all around, with dreadful consequences that echo down the centuries.

From Matthew 5:38–48 I would single out three extraordinary statements.

> As you know, we once were told "an eye for an eye and a tooth for a tooth," but I tell you: Do not react violently against the one who is evil. (38–39)

Jesus here denies the spiritual validity of an eye for an eye: he removes the right to engage in *violent* self-defense when an "evildoer" violates your humanity. Because someone wrongs you, you do not have the right to wrong your assailant. You may have the *power* to get even, but God does not give you the *right* to do so. Nor do you have the right to imitate the evil that led to the assault upon you. Again, you may have the power, but Jesus follows Amos in calling us away from the imitation of evil: "Seek good and not evil, that you may live.... Hate evil and love good, and establish justice in the gate" (Amos 5.14a and 15a).

The core precept here is not about passivity or flight. It is about fighting back with different weapons. It is about resisting the enemy without showing enmity. It is about higher-ground spirituality.

> As you know, we once were told, "You are to love your neighbor and you are to hate your enemy." But I tell you: Love your enemies. (43–44)

Here Jesus teaches that for those who would follow him, what might be called conventional loving is not enough. Such mundane, conventional loving is inadequate. What's more, the love we are to show our enemies is not really *about* the enemies. It is about God and about you as you begin to become a prism for the love and light of Jesus.

Some devotees of nonviolence speak of winning the friendship of the enemy. This in fact happens more than we know, in the serendipity of nonviolent or soul-force spirituality. You want to become a real child of God? The potential of the life within you is more than you know. Jesus says love your *enemies* and you will become that child of God. Becoming children of God happens only through the enlargement of our hearts by God's grace. But the practical consequence is that while we will continue to view the enemy as an enemy—remaining clear-sighted in that respect—we will also come to view that enemy as one of God's creatures and thereby deserving of our respect.

Moses insisted that the secret of the ethical life is to love God with one's whole being and whole energy. Moses likewise insisted that to love God in this way means to love the neighbor; he added that "neighbor" includes the alien and the stranger along with my other neighbors who are just like me and my kin. In our terms, the stranger Moses would have us love is the undocumented worker, arrived here in America from Ethiopia or Mexico. In the Mosaic scheme, the stranger we are to love is also by extension the person of another religion or the person of *no* religion: the atheist.

Jesus builds on this Mosaic continuum and completes it. Now "neighbor" also includes the *enemy*—the very person who wishes you harm or seeks to injure you.

Too many well-intentioned spiritual people do not believe there is any such thing as an enemy. I must differ. Among the people of this land are many who see *their* normalcy in terms of seeing *me* as a nonbeing.

KKK members and adherents of what is called Reconstruction Christianity see people of color as "mud people," created by a demon god of some kind. They do not believe people of color have the right to be alive and in this nation. According to them, we should be wiped out, exported, or enslaved.

The spiritual disease—still epidemic in our country—of seeing certain others as not being created of one blood is surely the worst form of evildoing imaginable. It is America's original sin—America's sin of sins. Some see women as "less than"; some see convicts on death row as deserving of death; some see working people as undeserving of even survival wages. And all of this diminishment of others shows an enmity toward life. It is an enmity that literally wastes people and kills people every day, but these deaths are invisible and unreported by our corporate media.

In the face of such death-dealing enmity, loving our enemies allows us, through God's grace, to break the cycle and to see and feel differently—to see and feel as God sees and feels. Loving our enemies stretches our imaginations so that the incredible and wonderful diversity of the human family becomes for us a thing of beauty and joy. Jesus teaches that in our process of becoming children of God, loving our enemies enables us to become as generous in grace as God is generous: that is, generous without limits.

This is the essence of the third extraordinary statement:

> God causes the sun to rise on both the bad and the good and sends rain to fall upon both the just and the unjust. (45)

The universe and all of creation, with so many mysteries that still lie far beyond our comprehension, makes room for every kind of life to flourish, permeated by grace. Because this grace has no limits, we who are followers of Jesus must love the enemy, for that enemy is the recipient of God's grace—of God's rain—just as we are. An awesome challenge, and an invitation direct from heaven to walk a better path.

Lord, plant my feet on higher ground!

When Love Is Stronger than Death: Making Peace One Heart at a Time

JOAN CHITTISTER

A new heart I will give you, and a new spirit I will put within you;
I will remove the heart of stone and give you a heart of flesh.

—*Ezekiel* 36:26

It is easy to talk about peace and peacemaking. It is another thing for even the most sincere people to make peace the priority of their lives in the midst of hostility. But I know it is possible because I have seen them do it.

I have watched people live in violence and give back love. I have seen them step tentatively across borders built to divide them and take an enemy hand, save an enemy property, hear an enemy story. What's more, I have seen it happen at the core of that most bitter and apparently intractable conflict of all—the conflict between Israeli occupation and Palestinian resistance, between Palestinian insurgency and Israeli resistance—whatever the history of the place, whatever the international agreements that say otherwise. The people go on—ahead of their governments, beyond the vision of their governments—not only in yearning for peace but in practicing it in small, important ways. And women are often the most active peacemakers of all.

Women's peacemaking is, without doubt, different from the peace processes followed by men. Women reach out to one other, to their children, to the personal needs of the people around them. Women do not seek to win a conflict. They seek to stop it. The world has a great deal to learn from the way women break through present fears and old resentments more readily, more openly than, history tells us, do the (mostly) male leaders who make peace at the end of a gun, who treat peacemaking as a matter of reaching formal agreements which, when they fail, only justify their going to war again.

These reflections, therefore, grow out of the extended experiences I had in Israel and Palestine in late 2003 and early 2004 as cochair of the Global Peace Initiative of Women Religious and Spiritual Leaders, a U.N. partnership organization. They are adapted from dispatches posted on the Web site of the *National Catholic Reporter* during that period. What I saw and heard in these visits invited me to confront again the teachings of Jesus, which so many fear, about disarming one's adversary by yielding and not retaliating—teachings that far too many theologians over the years have tried to evade or qualify out of existence. But the scripture is clear: "If anyone strikes you on the right cheek, turn the other also; and if anyone wants to sue you and take your coat, give your shirt as well; and if anyone forces you to go one mile, go also the second mile."

I watched women repeatedly walk the second mile.

What I saw did not lead me to suggest that persons already humiliated and victimized should be asked to be better and somehow nobler than their oppressors. On the contrary. The only way forward, it was clear, was for both sides, for everyone, at all levels—from ministers of government to motley crowds on the street—to surrender not their dignity but only the impulse to strike back.

I am also certain, having been there—and I say this with great sadness—that the everyday people of Palestine and Israel are much farther along in grasping this truth than are the American people, 90 percent of whom identify themselves as Christians but still see all-out war, and the death of many, as a necessary response against an entire people for the barbaric actions of the unauthorized few. And so the violence goes on.

When Stepping Backward Becomes a Step Forward

"One ought, every day at least," the poet Goethe wrote, " to hear a little song, read a good poem, see a fine picture, and, if it were possible, to speak a few reasonable words." I heard enough reasonable words in Israel and Palestine to last me for a long while. But I've spent many moments wondering if those words would possibly make any difference. I think they could; I'm not sure that they will. The problem is that they're too simple, too obvious, too true.

The group assembled in Jerusalem for a meeting of the World Council of Religious Leaders had about it the iconic air of sages and prophets. There were three swamis, two Buddhist monks, one rabbi, one Protestant bishop, and three nuns—a Buddhist, a Hindu, and a Catholic. Muslim imams, denied passage to the meeting, were conspicuous by their absence. It is possible that having been prevented from joining the group, they gained, in the end, an even more powerful presence.

Absent or present, the council members represented over five thousand years of holy books and spiritual texts and ascetic practices and meditation. But their talk was not about various meditation practices. Their talk was about the fruit of all that meditation.

This recently formed World Council of Religious Leaders had come to Israel and Palestine to assess, as wise and loving outsiders, what it was that religion itself could do to unravel the Gordian knot that blocks the coming of peace in the Middle East. The situation was delicate, the government said, and the meeting was inadvisable. The situation was urgent, the religious leaders said, and the meeting was imperative.

The religious women on the council, all cochairs of the Global Peace Initiative of Women, had already spent most of a week meeting with women from every dimension of Israeli-Palestinian society, listening to their experiences, trying to organize some kind of common cause among them. The men had arranged for listening sessions later in the week with major figures in both church and government. The two different but parallel approaches made for a complete but confusing perspective.

As the week progressed, the more complex the situation became. "Stop the occupation and we'll negotiate," the Palestinians insisted.

"Stop the bombings and we will listen," the Israelis shouted back. The standoff got clearer every day.

But every day another message came through as well: This was not a religious conflict, people told us over and over again. Instead, this was a political conflict that lacked religious leadership. The political issues were water and settlements, borders and security, viability and freedom. The religious issue, on the other hand, was how to understand the spiritual dimension of the problem in such a way that it would become imperative for the traditions involved to share an ancient land between two ancient peoples.

For over fifty years now, while all the other conflicts in the world have flared and died out again, this one has raged on. The question is why? Because foreign powers both created it and fuel it? Because international bodies have no stake in its resolution and so fail to resolve it? Because the people themselves do not want peace? Maybe.

But the religious leaders, having listened to all the issues, had a different word to say about it. They called for the kind of spiritual leadership that would lead people beyond religious justification of irreligious behavior. A swami commented, "Religion and ethnicity, culture and spirituality have become linked. Religion must be free of these."

A monk said, "We must call the religious leaders themselves to become together the voice of peace. They must find it among themselves and then they must lead their people to it."

The rabbi said, "Jacob and Esau must kiss again."

The bishop said, "These are cousins; this is a family squabble and only the family can end it."

A nun said, "In the struggle between Jacob and the angel, Jacob was wounded. Scripture says that 'Jacob limped.' Unless both these people are willing to live with a few wounds, unless they both give up insisting on the politically ideal situation, this struggle will never end."

At first blush, the conversation might have seemed to an observer to be, at best, a series of pious platitudes to be tolerated but never taken seriously. After all, what kind of politics is politics based on spiritual values?

Then, an older, seasoned dharma master from Taiwan who has lived in political tension all his life rose to speak. He folded his hands across his chest and said, slowly and distinctly, "a few reasonable words" to all the warring parties present: "When two people coming from two different directions try to cross a raging river on the same log in the same place at the same time," he said quietly, "the two of them will meet in the middle and neither can pass."

I thought to myself, "Well, that's exactly what we have here. This is the mother of all standoffs."

"Unless one of them backs up," the master went on, "neither can proceed."

But how do you convince one of them to back up, I thought to myself, when much of the satisfaction of the moment lies in winning the contest itself? Then came the Zen of the story.

"It is not easy to back up," the master sighed, "but it is the only way that both can cross the stream safely."

The real issue is not who is right and who is wrong, who got there first or who has right of passage. There is more than enough blame to go around in the Middle East. The real issue is not even the issues—all of which are resolvable. The real issue is whether or not some one of the parties will let go of "rights" for the sake of care.

The answer may be becoming clearer every day. The people are already trying to back up.

In the office of Yossi Belin, one of the Jewish architects of the Alternative Geneva Accords, work on bringing the society at large into the discussion of terms is intense. At least 40 percent of each population, surveys say, already supports the main ideas of the Geneva Accords: the recognition of the autonomy of both a Palestinian and Jewish state, the dismantling of Jewish settlements in Palestinian territory, the renunciation of Palestinian "right of return" to original homes and territories, and the dismantling of the apartheid wall.

From where I stand, there is no doubt about it. After fifty-five years of war, the people have had enough of the stalemate. The only question left is whether or not their governments, in the face of so much popular support for the Geneva Accords, will listen to the people.

"If the people will lead," the proverb says, "eventually the leaders will follow." We may discover any day now, while we "make the world safe for democracy," if that's still right. In the meantime, religious leadership and public support of the people's attempts to end a lifetime of madness is needed everywhere if the standoff on this global log is ever to end.

When Is a Barrier Not a Barrier?

I've never thought much about "the right of assembly." It was part of the Bill of Rights, I knew, but surely a less important one. Now I know better. One of the most implacable obstacles to Israeli-Palestinian negotiations remains freedom of movement or, to be more specific, the problem of the Palestinian checkpoints. Israelis fear that without these roadblocks suicide bombers will destroy Israel. In fact, over one thousand have already died.

Palestinians point out that the Israeli army has killed at least three times more Palestinians than the number of Israeli casualties incurred by bombers. But whatever the numbers, for now at least, thanks to the checkpoints, Israel has the dominant hand. Israelis move easily in and out of Palestinian territories while Palestinians can hardly move at all, even to their own villages.

The walling in of an entire people in retaliation for isolated attacks is a violation of the Geneva Conventions, which argue that group punishment, national punishment, for the crimes of a few is itself an illegal act. But the checkpoints remain. They are a daily irritation, a daily threat to human dignity and a mockery of human trust.

Palestine is being treated as if it were a foreign country but given none of the rights of a foreign country—the right to make treaties or develop alliances or regulate airspace. Instead, documentation and entry permits are required on a day-to-day basis for women to shop and men to go to work on the other side of the "border" and for families to come and go between the two territories to visit a grandmother on one side, a sister on the other. Worse, things such as these can't be done at all if one can't get a permit.

As a result, at least thirty infant deaths have been reported at checkpoints because their pregnant mothers did not have a permit to cross that day and could not get to a hospital.

Brothers are separated from brothers in nearby villages because those territories, still under Israeli control, are not open areas.

So contentious is the checkpoint question that Israeli women themselves monitor the most trafficked of the crossover stations to document cases of intimidation—or, on the other hand, to defend young Israeli soldiers against charges of brutality.

Now here I was in the midst of the situation, going through these very same checkpoints myself in order to work with women on both sides of the border. Which is how I discovered how easy it is to become a smuggler.

Our hope was that in the course of the meeting of the World Council of Religious Leaders we would be able as well to spend a few hours with one of the Palestinian participants in the Global Peace Initiative of Women. We also wanted to visit some of the holy sites. It was a pleasant happenstance. She taught at Bethlehem University; we wanted to visit the Church of the Nativity there. All we had to do to get there, we were told, was to take a cab.

Our Arab driver was a bright man, a father of four children under the age of twelve and the holder of a degree in archaeology. But archaeological digs had become irregular since hostilities had increased. To support his family, he was driving a cab now. Since he had a Jerusalem work permit, he could take us to Bethlehem, stay with us for the afternoon, and bring us back. He was happy for the fare. It would be a twenty-minute ride.

But then we hit one of the movable checkpoints that crop up without warning in the area. "There are a hundred cars ahead of us," our driver said. "We can't go this way or you will never get back to Jerusalem in time for your meeting tonight. I will go another way." He gunned the car out of the line, spun us around, and headed back in the opposite direction. "Crazy," I thought. "Bethlehem is a straight shot down this highway. Where could we possibly be going?"

A mile or two from the checkpoint, the cabbie pulled the car over to the side of the road, parked in another line of empty cars, and told us to wait in the locked car. He would "check the other side," he said. And disappeared. When he showed up again, there was a smile on his face. He was standing on the crest of the hill in front of us and waving us forward.

It was not a very high climb, but it was not an easy one either. I hung on to his arm on the path and let him pull me up the incline. Part of the hill was mud, the other rock. People had clearly gone this way before us; the mud was packed into clay. But the way was anything but defined, anything but clear. There were no signs, no real road, no clue of connections.

Yet there, on the other side of the rise, was another line of empty cabs. Our cabbie gave his car keys to one of the drivers there and went with us to another cab, which carried a Palestinian license plate. We were now on the way to Bethlehem on back roads, through villages, behind and around and beyond the checkpoint. We were smugglers, in other words, in a very well-organized culture of smugglers.

But Bethlehem was dark and empty. A few shopkeepers sat in dark stores waiting for people who did not know how to smuggle themselves in. Most of the vendors had never bothered to open their stores at all. Over 70 percent of the people of Bethlehem, we were told, are unemployed. When we returned the same way hours later, we picked up a woman and her daughter who had also climbed the hill to smuggle themselves into Bethlehem. They had come to see the woman's mother and, if necessary, intended to walk over the hills again to get back home. Much in the style of Jesus, Mary, and Joseph on the way to Egypt, I imagine.

Then, on the way down the highway in the dark, I noticed three boys dart across a six-lane highway, jumping barriers as they went, until they disappeared through a garden gate that spanned both sides of the next checkpoint another hundred yards away. They were smuggling themselves around the Israelis, too, the driver told us—on the way to see their families or their friends—or maybe their girlfriends.

Smuggling had become a way of life here, the driver told us. There was no other way. His own cousin, he told us, had done it to see his aging parents the month before, but he had not been so lucky then as we were today. Discovered without papers at a random checkpoint, his cousin had been jailed and the cab, his only livelihood, impounded for a month.

From where I stand, "the right of assembly" has taken on new meaning. Clearly it is a fundamental human right. It has everything to do with forging a nation, sustaining its families and organizing its people. In the meantime, to deny it is only to stoke the smoldering fires of enmity, give support to more terrorism, and retard even more the coming of peace. Surely this is not security. Surely there must be a better way.

Treaties Don't Do It; Homes Do

Governments wage both war and peace on paper. Real people, on the other hand, bear the brunt of both.

Governments plan "strategic attacks" and—in Iraq, at least—never even bother to count the bodies they leave behind. Nor do they ever count the mothers or children or young wives or old fathers who suddenly find themselves standing alongside the corpses of those whose death leaves them without a future, bereft of a past by the death of their loved ones.

Governments also make peace on paper. They divide territories, whole countries, tribes, clans, and families and sign treaties to ratify the divisions. But the treaties do not work. Long after the writing on the paper fades, the war goes on in the hearts of those whose lives were silently smothered by it.

In our own time, they have done it in Germany, Korea, Africa, and Israel-Palestine. Arbitrary land grabs—conceived in small dark rooms and large conference halls by men who have never even walked the territory, let alone lived there, left relatives there, built there, or buried their dead there—leave scars that never heal on the streets and villages where peace really counts.

Hutus and Tutsis in Rwanda rage at each other over lost tribal territories. Koreans weep at the border and threaten one another with a new generation of Koreans who stand toe to toe, promising to annihilate cousins they have never met. Germans died in no-man's-land in East Berlin, attempting to reunite with family members on the other side of town.

In Israel, a 750-km wall costing $1 million a kilometer separates farmers from their chickens, families from their olive groves. "They make a desert," the Roman philosopher Seneca said, "and call it peace." But it is those who have lost their lands, have been divided from their families, in whom the war never ends and for whom peace never comes.

In Israel, I discover, it is unusually easy to become embroiled in the game of who's right and who's wrong. The Jewish people need a homeland, yes. The Palestinians rejected the 1948 U.N. mandate that decreed that, yes.

The Palestinians need a homeland, yes. The Israelis refuse to recognize that, yes.

The Israelis hesitate even to put their children on a school bus, yes. The Arabs, minus the political rights of a sovereign nation, are insecure even in their homes, yes.

The Israelis are living in fear, yes. The Palestinians are living in fear, yes.

Both peoples want peace, yes. Both governments refuse to negotiate it, yes.

When both governments do negotiate, both peoples lose, and which side is "right" begins to blur. I saw it with my own eyes.

Basma, the attractive and lively young Palestinian woman who acted as a kind of local secretary to the U.N.-initiated Global Peace Initiative of Women, met us at our meeting sites every morning in the same clothes. It took four days before I realized that Basma didn't have any other clothes. Her fourteen-apartment housing complex had been bulldozed the week before because Israeli soldiers had reason to believe that a suspected terrorist had run into the building for refuge. They killed the suspect and then bulldozed the building anyway. No residents were allowed to retrieve anything from the building before it was leveled. Basma had no clothes, no books, no records, nothing now. And yet, every morning she came to work for peace.

On the other hand, we visited the planned city of Ariel on the top of a mountain in Samaria, one of Israel's West Bank settlements. When Ariel's first settlers arrived there thirty years ago, in 1975, the mountaintop was bare. Now it is a city of eighteen thousand inhabitants, nine thousand of whom are immigrants from Russia. It is a gleaming new development, sparklingly clean, completely "built by these ten fingers," as one woman put it.

Ariel is a totally wireless college town of over ten thousand students —thanks to one woman's investment of $18 million—and a center for the development of laser crystals and medical research. There are 120 factories in Ariel that employ over six thousand people, two thousand of them Arab. Rethink the word *settlement*. In 1992, with the freezing of settlements on the West Bank, all construction in Ariel stopped. Now the city park, the sports complex, and the cultural center are empty shells of a city whose evolution was stopped in mid-flight in a settlement initially planned to be home for sixty thousand to eighty thousand people. If present peace plans are ever completed, Ariel will be one of the settlements dismantled or left to Palestinian control.

"We used to have good relationships with our Arab neighbors. I miss them," one woman said.

Another said, "I helped build this city from the ground up. It is our biblical right. After all, the prophet Jeremiah said, 'The time will come when you will plant vineyards on the mountains of Samaria.'"

A third woman explained, "I've lived here over twenty years. I love every inch of it. I have as much right to live here as anyone does to live in Haifa. Why Ariel for peace; why not Tel Aviv for peace?"

Lena, born in Russia, came to Ariel in 1991. "This is the only place Jews can live. We want peace, but we may have to sacrifice [our children] to get it.... I'm not ready to sacrifice our land."

Jewish women, all longtime members of the Israeli peace movement, sat quietly and listened to the women from Ariel. "We do not seek agreements," they said. "We seek understanding of each other through personal encounters, through humanizing the dispute, through a search for common ground." Three members of the group, all women rabbis, will go back every month to hold discussion groups with the women of Ariel.

Margaret Thatcher said once, "In politics, if you want anything said, ask a man. If you want anything done, ask a woman."

All the treaties written and proclaimed in government Rose Gardens have yet to work. From where I stand, it looks like it may be only these women—one displaced Palestinian girl, one group of Arab-Israeli women—working together to save one another's homes who can ever get beyond politics to peace.

Back in the hotel meeting rooms, I saw a young Jewish mother hand her baby to a blind Palestinian woman while she rose to talk about the uselessness of peace treaties and the need for common public actions that would say a decisive no to war. Looking at the two of them, totally unconscious of the gap in culture and concerns they had bridged by that very act, I knew that the work had already begun.

When Playground Politics Don't Work, What Then?

Independence and autonomy survive generation after generation as central American virtues. We start teaching them to our children in kindergarten. The first time an American child balks at going back to school or begs a parent, preferably a father, to go with him or her because of fear of being pushed in the playground, more often than not they get good American counsel. "You have to learn to take care of yourself," we tell them. "If anyone pushes you, you just push them back. Harder."

The teaching shows signs of having application at much higher levels later on in life, which is a sign of very effective teaching indeed. "Playground politics," I call it. "Defense," they call it.

Here's how it works: When someone collapses your towers, you go collapse their country, its electrical grids, its government, its water supplies, its economy. No justification necessary beyond "push harder." When the weapons of mass destruction you worried about aren't there, no problem. When there isn't—and never was—an imminent danger, don't let a little thing like that concern you. When the conspiracy of evil between your enemies and this government, as you argued, is not only missing but entirely bogus, don't worry. Just begin to talk about punishing the bully in the playground and you're safe.

Examining the history of public acquiescence to military involvement, one finds that we like the playground reason best of all. We buy it over and over again: We bought it in Vietnam, in Chile, in Guatemala, in Iraq. No logic necessary. No one questions why we shove some international bullies but not others.

It's the old "That'll show 'em, bring 'em on" argument. And it is, apparently, enough.

It makes us feel good. It renews our sense of American invulnerability even though nobody thinks we're invulnerable anymore, not even the people who do the pushing. We know that because they have given us a color code of anxiety levels to prove it. Which makes you wonder whether or not pushing back harder really solves anything. Worse, it makes you wonder, doesn't it, whatever happened to the "independence, autonomy, and freedom" that playground politics purports to restore?

We're not the only people who respond like this, of course. But with our high-tech weapons and our high-tech profits, we do it bigger and better and on a far larger scale than most. At least shock and awe seems to work, until our laser weapons prove to be useless in the fight between helicopters and shoulder-fired missiles, or between canister bombs and tanks without a target, or between the uprisings of the people and a rising of the deficit that threatens to make the money run out before the insurgency does. Which, given the size of the new deficit, it apparently has.

Then we need something far more meaningful than the perception of defense to defend us, something far more powerful than hate to bring us peace. What we surely do not need is more of the same.

But there is hope. I have seen it happen, so I know it can. In the midst of chaos, some people refuse to add to it.

In Israel, the apartheid wall that will lock one people inside an artificial area to keep bombs out of another artificial area is rising quickly. It has begun to separate the Arab section of an ancient part of Jerusalem itself from the remainder of the city.

The wall is clearly an attempt at invulnerability, too. People all around the world are watching the spectacle of its construction, some in disbelief, others in horror, all of them in confusion. Sensible, temperate people wince at the thought of walling in an entire population—but, they reason, if it stops suicide bombings of buses and malls and restaurants, it may be the best thing to do. For everybody's sake, right?

But there are drawbacks to the search for invulnerability. The bombing may stop, but the hatred deepens for other reasons. Now, while the wall is still being built, old Arab women are climbing over it to get to the markets, but it won't be long before the wall is too high, too wide, too wired to attempt anything like that anymore. The checkpoints, the borders that separate families will get more difficult to cross. Then the seething will still go on, of course, but hopefully it will be contained in its own territory. Hopefully.

Yet there is one dimension of human life that seems to go on long past physical ability. Human memory is the long, long excursion of the heart into the past. It passes down from one generation to the next, from the Crusades to the Twin Towers, from Ishmael to Arafat, from Isaac to Sharon.

There is only one thing that can cure someone of a bad memory, and that is to put a better one in its place. All the time the tanks are rumbling and the bombs are exploding on each side of the wall, there are people there making other memories on which the future might well feed.

Leila, a blind Palestinian woman, a therapist, goes in and out of Gaza, making friends with Israeli border guards as she goes. She tells them stories, sings them songs, smiles at them in the internal brightness of her darkness and refuses to hate. At the same time, the Rabbis for Peace, an organization of Israeli rabbis who are devoted to stopping the hate and so stopping the war, make friends with Arab families, rebuild the Arab homes bulldozed by the Israeli army, and pick the olives that will sustain the families of Arab farmers who are separated by the wall from their olive groves. They do Arab work on the Israeli side.

Love, the scripture tells us, is stronger than death.

Standing within a roomful of Israeli and Arab women who want to work together for peace, it becomes clearer every day that love is also stronger than walls, stronger than bullies, stronger even than the people who push back harder.

Now if we would only teach that to children in kindergarten, we might not have such a hard time later convincing the people who start the wars to make the world safe for democracy that playground politics are a very short-term solution to anything. Then maybe we would really be invulnerable. Then maybe we could really feel good again.

Easter Faith and Empire: Recovering the Prophetic Tradition on the Emmaus Road

CHED MYERS

And Abraham said to the rich man, "If they don't listen to Moses and the prophets, neither will they be convinced even if someone rises from the dead."

—*Luke* 16:31

In the first-century Pax Romana, Christians had the difficult and demanding task of discerning how to cling to a radical ethos of life—symbolized preeminently by their stubborn belief in the Resurrection of Jesus—while living under the chilling shadow of an imperial culture of domination and death. Today, in the twenty-first-century Pax Americana, U.S. Christians are faced with the same challenge: to celebrate Easter faith in the teeth of empire and its discontents.

"The words *empire* and *imperialism* enjoy no easy hospitality in the minds and hearts of most contemporary Americans," wrote the great historian William Appleman Williams a quarter century ago in his brilliant rereading of U.S. history.[1] Yet today, because of the ascendancy of the New Right's ideological project (whose intellectual architecture is typified by the Project for a New American Century), the words are increasingly used approvingly in regard to U.S. policy. We are indeed well down the road of imperial unilateralism, and are seeing clearly that this means a world held hostage to wars and rumors of war. The conquest and occupation of Afghanistan and Iraq have had an enormous human and political cost. Meanwhile, the United States has military bases on every continent and some form of military presence in almost two-thirds of the 189 member states in the United Nations.

Williams believed that "we have only just begun our confrontation with our imperial history, our imperial ethic, and our imperial psychology. . . . Americans of the 20th century like empire for the same reasons their ancestors had favored it in the 18th and 19th centuries. It provides them with renewable opportunities, wealth, and other benefits and satisfactions including a psychological sense of well being and power."[2]

Predictably, in the religious sphere, a brand of Christianity that fits hand in glove with imperial America is flourishing. It is a discouraging time indeed for those in our churches who are distressed by the manipulative religious rhetoric and posturing of the Bush administration.

To combat this disastrous drift, we need to turn to deeper sources of critique and hope. I believe our scriptural tradition offers such resources for our struggle to recover a nonimperial faith and to imagine a nonimperial future. But we must wrest these sacred stories back from the clutches of the religious Right, offering a more compelling reading. This essay means to be a small contribution to this task.

Chocolate-Coating Easter in Wartime

For the churches of the Northern Hemisphere, the fact that Eastertide is celebrated in the heart of springtime has been a mixed blessing. On one hand, there is a powerful resonance between this season of surging new life in nature and the story of Christ's Resurrection. On the other, the liturgical and theological meaning of Easter has often been lost amid other, more popular rites of spring. For Christians in the United States, however, our greatest problem in this present moment of war is the omnipresent temptation to conflate Easter's story of God's power over death with the triumphalistic pretensions of omnipotence that characterize American empire.

I write on the second anniversary of the declared "end" to the latest Iraq war, called by the Bush administration Operation Iraqi Freedom, but more accurately referred to in Britain as the Fifth Anglo-Iraq War. But that war rages on, and as of this moment some ten times more U.S. servicemen and -women have lost their lives during the ensuing occupation than during the official hostilities. And though it is official Bush administration policy *not* to tally the Iraqi soldiers, insurgents, and civilians killed in this latest conflict—"We don't do body counts," as General Tommy Franks put it—the number is estimated to be anywhere between twenty-five thousand and one hundred thousand.

Statistics, however, don't have the power to move our hearts and minds. For this, a recent story must suffice to bring home the cruelty of this war. On April 16, 2005, Californian Marla Ruzicka and her Iraqi colleague Faiz Ali Salim were killed when their car was caught between a suicide car bomber and a U.S. military convoy. Marla was the founder of the Campaign for Innocent Victims in Conflict (CIVIC) in 2003, an NGO that began as a one-woman operation and grew to include dedicated Iraqis who compiled statistics of Iraqi civilian casualties. Marla and her colleagues pursued this difficult, heart-wrenching job by going door-to-door in a country that has already sent most other aid agencies packing.

In an obituary in the *Christian Science Monitor* Jill Carroll wrote that Ruzicka

> made a name for herself working for Global Exchange, the U.S. organization that sent field workers to Afghanistan to count civilian casualties. After the Iraq war, she moved her push for an accurate count of civilian casualties to Baghdad. At a time when the International Committee of the Red Cross and United Nations were leaving Iraq, Marla started CIVIC. Through that, she helped Iraqi families navigate the process of claiming compensation from the U.S. military for injuries and deaths. When she died Marla was traveling to visit some of the many Iraqi families she was working to help. . . . She would point out, this happens to Iraqis every day and no one notices or even cares. There are no newspaper articles or investigations into what happens to them. For most of them, there was only Marla.[3]

The tragic fate of such an advocate for justice invites thoughtful Christians to come to terms with the Shadow of Death, *especially* in the midst of Eastertide.

Unfortunately, our churches are not particularly adept at navigating such difficult and distressing terrain. Instead, we tend to sugarcoat—or should I say chocolate-cover—this highest of Christian holy days, burying it under flowers and swelling hymns and egg hunting. Our public theology of Easter is, consequently, experiencing diminishing returns. We have forgotten that the Resurrection accounts in our gospels *themselves* took place under the Shadow of Death. It is because these Bible stories narrate a real world like our own that they can offer us true hope to resist the reign of death, rather than some sort of religious inoculation against its consequences. To recover this tough character of our scriptures, however, demands a little recontextualization.

Let us take as an example Luke's famous account of the road to Emmaus—perhaps the church's most traditional and beloved Easter text (Luke 24:13ff). This moving story narrates a conversation between an unrecognized Jesus and two obscure disciples. As the exchange along the road makes perfectly clear, Jesus's execution presented a crushing blow to the movement he founded—a chilling Shadow of Death. Nevertheless, this little vignette has managed to become profoundly sentimentalized in our churches, every bit as domesticated by our pious traditions as the Last Supper story.

"When thoughts turn to the Last Supper," one art critic has said, "we seem to see only Leonardo da Vinci's representation before us." The Upper Room appears as a serene moment of beatific communion in a chapel-like setting. But this image, so deeply ingrained in our religious consciousness, could not be further from the scene narrated in the gospels. What we find there is a frantic, furtive, and clandestine gathering of hunted fugitives on the verge of nervous breakdowns hiding out in the attic of a safe house. The scene is held together only by a determined Jesus, even though he knows these companions will abandon him when the authorities come after him, as they inevitably will.[4]

A similar chocolate covering obscures the road to Emmaus. It exists in popular churchly imagination as a contemplative stroll through a shaded landscape, a casual tête-à-tête delightfully interrupted by the

Risen Lord (think, for example, of the famous religious painting by Swiss Pietist artist Robert Zund [1827–1909], in which the warm and tranquil scene looks as if it was concocted by the Hudson River School of romantic art). The scenario portrayed in Luke's gospel, however, is far more suggestive of present-day Iraq. Only forty-eight hours earlier Jesus of Nazareth had been summarily executed by the Roman military, in a fashion all too familiar to Palestinian Jews of the time: as a dissident prosecuted for resisting the "occupying authority." A little narrative common sense, therefore, would suggest that the two disciples in our story would be neither leisurely nor calmly reflective at this particular moment. Rather, they would be on the lam, hustling down a back road, getting the hell out of Dodge so they won't meet the same fate as their leader.

Hustling Down the Emmaus Back Road

What does the text tell us about these coconspirators trying to "melt into the countryside" (as the Pentagon routinely says of Iraqi insurgents)? Their destination is interesting: Emmaus, a village (in Greek, *koomee*) so obscure that it receives no other mention in the scriptures. There are no fewer than four different traditions concerning its location, ranging from four to twenty miles outside Jerusalem. Emmaus is attested to elsewhere only in two ancient sources:

- In the book of Maccabees it is a site where the vastly outnumbered Jewish guerillas heroically defeated the Syrian invaders (I Maccabees 3:40–4:15).
- Josephus notes that the victorious Roman emperor Vespasian, just a few years after vanquishing the Judean revolt in 70 AD, made a political point by settling eight hundred Roman military veterans at "a place called Emmaus" (Wars VII:6:6).

These references suggest that our little village had a reputation for homegrown resistance, which the empire later felt some need to control by turning it into a military colony. (Such a scenario is certainly familiar to our own imperial context.)

As our disciples are "hightailing it for the border" so they can lay low for a while, Luke tells us they "were discussing all the things that had happened" (24:14). No doubt! This was likely an animated conversation between labored breaths and anxious glances over their shoulders. They were probably blaming each other for the mess they'd gotten into, wondering what their next move might be, lamenting Roman kangaroo justice, cursing the colonizers, even cursing Jesus for failing to deliver on his promises of a new social order. They had a *lot* to talk about, but this was no peripatetic philosophical wander. Rather, this was a grief-laden, scared stiff, and contentious debriefing under the Shadow of Death.

Though one would never imagine the scene this way based on our tradition of religious art, a couple of simple exegetical notes confirm my suspicions. First, the distinctively Lukan verb for "to discuss" in verses 14 and 15 is *homīlien,* from which we get our term *homiletics*. It appears only two other times in the New Testament, both in Acts:

- In Acts 20:11 it describes Paul's sobering farewell sermon at Troas, a serious through-the-night conversation about how the young movement would survive.

- In Acts 24:26 it refers to Paul's conversations with the Roman governor Felix concerning "justice, self-control and coming judgment," a discussion, we are told, that scared the ruler to death.

Homīlien refers to weighty matters, then, not philosophizing removed from real-world consequences. Moreover, in the New Testament the verb *suzeetein* almost always connotes a passionate dispute, while the phrase "all the things that had happened" in Luke 24:14 refers elsewhere specifically to the arrest, trial, and execution of Jesus or to parallel sufferings of disciples.

The disciples' preoccupation with this intense and even desperate discussion may explain why they didn't immediately recognize their teacher. Or, as Daniel Berrigan has suggested, perhaps they didn't know Jesus because he was so beat up and disfigured by his torturers. Indeed, Luke tells us later in his account that the Risen Jesus's scars were still visible (Luke 24:39), and after all, tradition holds that he'd "been to hell and back." Or it may be that Luke is working here in the midrashic traditions of the "incognito Second Coming"; the rabbis often speculated that the prophet Elijah would return anonymously to see if the world was ready to receive him.

In any case, the Stranger's response makes it clear that he has walked in on a heated debate, for 24:17 reads literally: "'What words were you throwing back and forth at each other [Greek, *antiballete*, here only in the New Testament] while you were making your way?' And they looked gloomy [Greek, *skuthroopoi*]." Jesus perceives them as struggling with each other and in a bad mood. And Cleopas's retort betrays a distinct tone of impatience: "So are you the *only* one in Jerusalem who doesn't know what's been going down these last few days?" he asks dryly (24:18). Or maybe he is exhibiting a wary defensiveness. They are fugitives, and who is this unknown person asking prying questions?

Now that Luke has established sufficient angst in the scene, we can detect a certain delicious irony in how the Stranger plays dumb (given what he's just been through). "Huh??!!" he says with a straight face (24:19a). "Do tell!" Cleopas, passionately if a bit recklessly, launches in to the whole sordid affair: how Jesus of Nazareth had resuscitated the prophetic tradition, igniting hope in people longing for shalom. And how *his own* leaders (bloody collaborators!) had railroaded him and sold him out to the imperial oppressors, who strung him up (24:19b–20). Finally his frustration boils over: "And we had *trusted* [Greek, *eelpizomen*] that he was the One to liberate Israel" (24:21). His bitter disappointment, his sense of betrayal, his confusion is palpable.

It is not difficult to feel empathy for Cleopas here. He had staked his life on the hope that *this* messianic movement, unlike so many others in recent generations, would finally break the yoke of oppression that had strangled his people for centuries. He'd committed himself to the risky business of challenging the native aristocracy and their imperial overlords. But things had turned out all wrong. Jesus's march on Jerusalem (Luke 19:28ff) had not resulted in a popular uprising, but instead had come crashing down in a vicious counterinsurgent thrust by the colonizers. Their leader had been publicly executed, and they had fled for their lives, an all points bulletin hanging over their heads.

And if that weren't enough, miserable Cleopas concludes his sad tale by relating, with apparent aggravation, a rumor circulating among some of his dispirited companions—*women's* rumors, mind you—about visions of angels and an empty tomb (24:22–24). The authorities had probably hijacked Jesus's body, everything was falling apart, the movement was in disarray, and they'd been arguing about it all day, and frankly, *he'd had it*.

It shouldn't be difficult for modern Americans to imagine this traumatized scene. Think of how civil rights activists were feeling on April 6, 1968, in Memphis, Tennessee. (Here another image comes to mind: the famous photo taken of the balcony of the Lorrain Motel the moment after King was shot on April 4, 1968. Three men stand over King's body, frantically gesturing toward the shooter, while one—revealed later to be a government agent—kneels beside King.) We'd better believe that Martin Luther King's lieutenants were going crazy trying to figure out what *really* had gone down two days before, why and how their leader had been gunned down, who was behind it, what it meant for the movement, and whether they might be next on the hit list.

This is the real world of COINTELPRO and conspiracy, of imperial "justice" meted out by good old boys who can hardly contain their glee at the prophet's demise, of stern calls for law and order in the wake of this "tragedy" by the very ones who engineered it. It is the world of popular movements on the verge of a major social impact being aborted in the face of state repression.

This was hardly a stroll in the park. But it is *this* world that Luke's story also inhabits, not the fantasy world we so often imagine in our churches. We North American Christians rarely grapple with such matters: we are too preoccupied with institutional survival to entertain the possibility that our whole nation might be captive to the same powers that took out Jesus and King. We talk about "power in the name of Jesus" but are too timid to interrogate public addiction or high corporate crimes. We speculate blithely about the "last days" while endorsing world-historic shifts in U.S. military and economic policies that are chewing up millions of the lives *we* say God loves, and that are destroying the land and sea and air *we* say God created, and that are usurping the glory *we* say belongs to God alone. We are content to keep our heads down and examine the finer points of doctrine or liturgy or church demographics, well insulated from the Shadow of Death.

Jesus, on the other hand, as portrayed in Luke's beautiful story, *embraces* the trauma. His response to Cleopas is instructive. He doesn't scold them for mixing religion and politics, nor does he redirect them to turn inward to a life of the spirit, nor does he console them with pat theories of history. Instead, he walks with these poor boys for a few miles, inquiring, listening to their pain. And then he responds with, of all things, *a Bible study* (something that makes modern theological liberals blush yet hardly fits in the hermeneutic program of conservatives). To be precise, the first recorded Bible study in the life of an Easter church that hasn't even been birthed yet at Pentecost. "OK, fellas," Jesus says, "it's a bad time, alright. So open your Bibles to the prophets and let's reread history together under the Shadow of Death."

Reading History through the Prophets

Luke tells us that Jesus addresses these fit-to-be-tied disciples as "fools" (24:25). But the Greek term *anontoi* refers simply to those who don't quite get it, who find the truth as yet unintelligible (cf. Romans 1:14; Galatians 3:1, 3). He knows their hearts are "sluggish" (Greek, *bradeis*), as indeed are ours. Because we, like Cleopas and company, forever refuse to embrace the counterintuitive wisdom of the Hebrew prophets.

The prophets tell us to defend the poor, but we lionize the rich. The prophets tell us that horses and chariots cannot save us, but we are transfixed by the apparent omnipotence of modern military technology. The prophets tell us to forgo idolatry, but we compulsively fetishize the work of our own hands. Above all, the prophets warn us that the way to liberation in a world locked down by the spiral of violence, the way to redemption in a world of enslaving addictions, the way to true transformation in a world of deadened conscience and numbing conformity is the way of nonviolent, sacrificial, creative love. But we who are slow of heart—a euphemism for not having courage—instead remain fiercely loyal to ever more fabulous myths of redemptive violence, practices of narcissism, and delusions of our own nobility.

And what we balk at most is the Stranger's punch line, the watershed query upon which our theological reading of history hangs: "Was it not necessary [Greek, *edei*] that Messiah should suffer?" (24:26). This is the imperfect form of a technical apocalyptic term that appears throughout the New Testament. It refers to the fact that an official reaction to prophetic witness is *inevitable*. This is *not* a rhetorical question for Christological catechizing about cosmic propitiation, the way traditional atonement theories have it. It is the rather the ultimate challenge to our deepest assumptions about society and the cosmos, the taproot counterassertion that unmasks our profound captivity to the logic of domination and retributive justice. The prophet's death is not *necessary*, given the character of God; it is, however, *inevitable*, given the character of the state. No one who pays attention to history can dispute the truth of this assertion.

Because North Americans keep wanting the good guys to win, we are forced to make believe that even the worst sort of characters are the good guys. We strive to manage history from the top down, to control it with our technologies, to win all battles with overwhelming power. And the prophets keep talking about revolution from the bottom up, the wisdom of outsiders, the power of the least. Like the disciples in Luke's story, we Christians understand enough to acknowledge that Jesus lived a prophet's life, but not enough to recognize the historically redemptive power of his prophet's death.

"Then beginning with Moses and all the prophets he interpreted to them the scriptures" (24:27). The verb is *dieermeeneuen*; every other time it appears in the New Testament it means "to translate into one's native tongue" (Acts 9:36), including the interpretation of ecstatic languages (I Corinthians 12:30, 14:5, 13:27). In other words, Jesus is patiently translating this counterintuitive biblical wisdom into the plainest possible terms so these demoralized disciples can get it. And that, I want to suggest, is what the task of our Easter theological reflection should be about under the Shadow of Death.

More than any other gospel writer, Luke portrays Jesus as using Israel's prophets for his own interpretive lens:

- "God has raised up a mighty savior for us . . . as spoken through the mouth of God's holy *prophets* from of old, that we would be saved from our enemies and from the hand of all who hate us." (Luke 1:69–71)

- Jesus stood up to read and the scroll of the *prophet* Isaiah was given to him. . . . And Jesus said, "Truly I tell you, no *prophet* is accepted in the prophet's hometown." (4:17, 27)

- "Blessed are you when people hate you, and when they exclude you, revile you, and defame you on account of the Human One . . . for that is what their ancestors did to the *prophets*." (6:22-23)

- They glorified God, saying, "A great *prophet* has risen among us!" . . . "What did you go out to see? A *prophet*? Yes, and more than a *prophet*." (7:16, 26)

- The disciples answered, "Some say you are John the Baptist; others, Elijah; and still others, that one of the ancient *prophets* has arisen." (9:19)

- "There will be weeping and gnashing of teeth when you see Abraham and Isaac and Jacob and all the *prophets* in the kingdom of God, and you thrown out. . . . Yet today, tomorrow, and the next day I must be on my way, because it is impossible for a *prophet* to be killed outside of Jerusalem." (13:28, 33-34)

- Jesus took the twelve aside and said, "See, we are going up to Jerusalem, and everything that is written about the Human One by the *prophets* will be accomplished." (18:31)

These prophets are the ones who throughout the national history engaged the way things *were* with the vision of what *could* and *should* be. They question authority, make trouble, refuse to settle, interrupt business as usual, speak truth to power, give voice to the voiceless. They stir up the troops, get the natives restless, picket presidential palaces, question foreign policies based on military and economic domination—and are accused of treason in times of national war making.

For being the inconvenient conscience of the nation the prophets are jailed or exiled or killed—and then, once safely disposed of, they get a national holiday or a street named after them. Once canonized, they are thereafter ignored by their public patrons. Luke's Jesus makes this point crystal clear in his tirade against such officials:

> Woe to you scribes! For you build the tombs of the prophets whom your ancestors killed. So you are witnesses and approve of the deeds of your ancestors; for they killed them, and you build their tombs. Therefore also the Wisdom of God said, "I will send them prophets and apostles, some of whom they will kill and persecute" . . . from the blood of Abel to the blood of Zechariah." (Luke 11:47–51)

What was true then "from A to Z" continues now from Sitting Bull to Martin Luther King. Nevertheless, it is the prophets themselves—*not* their corporate-sponsored hagiographies—who teach us how our collective story should be read, says the Stranger. Their witness, however maligned by those in power, represents the hermeneutic key to the whole tradition. And that's why it was *inevitable* that Messiah would follow in their footsteps.

Whose Shock, Whose Awe?

In the first half of the Emmaus story, the inaugural appearance of the Risen Christ is in the form of a Stranger. But in the second half of the story, he is famously revealed in the breaking of the bread (Luke 24:28–32). In the middle of that episode, after Jesus has vanished, the two disciples exclaim, "Were not our hearts burning within us while he was talking to us on the road, while he was opening the scriptures to us?" (24:32). The verb "to open up" (Greek, *dianoigo*) in other appearances in the gospels refers to the opening of deaf ears (Mark 7:34-35), of a closed womb (Luke 2:23), of blind eyes (Luke 24:31), and of a hardened heart (Acts 16:14). The only other time it is employed in relation to the scriptures is when Paul struggles to persuade his synagogue compatriots that "it was *inevitable* that Jesus had to suffer" (Acts 17:3). This underlines the point of the Emmaus road conversation: our perspective on traumatic historic events is not ultimately a matter of rational persuasion but of opening blind eyes and deaf ears and hard hearts to the difficult truth of discipleship under the Shadow of Death. And when our hearts are truly opened, they will burn with renewed commitment.

With this jolt of recognition/revelation, the narrative reverses directions. The fugitive disciples now return to the capital city to face its dangers (24:33a). The next scene (24:33b–36) shows the Emmaus road pair relating their experience to the other disciples. Jesus appears again to the whole group, and Luke reports that they were "afraid and awestruck" (24:37).

These two Greek adjectives are worth noting. The first is *ptoeoo*, which means in the active mood "to terrify," and in the passive mood (used here) "to be terrified." The only other time it appears in the New Testament is in Luke 21:9: "When you hear of wars and upheavals, do not be terrified; these things are *inevitable.*" It is understandable that these disciples would be horrified: crucifixion was the preeminent form of Roman state terrorism. This gruesome form of public execution—reserved for political dissidents—had only one function: to intimidate those in the occupied territories in the name, of course, of imperial "national security." It was a very effective way of broadcasting the message: "Look what happens to those who think they can challenge the sovereignty of Caesar."

But the other adjective is *emphobos,* which in the New Testament is reserved for connoting awe in presence of God or of the Risen Christ. So these disciples were on one hand cowering before a dreadful state, yet on the other were reeling before the unimaginable possibility that Rome's ultimate form of social control had not defeated Jesus. Why does the prospect of his Resurrection generate such strong reaction here? *Not* because corpse resuscitation upset the laws of nature—that's a problem only for modern folk, and it mostly generates skepticism. No, the Resurrection was overwhelming to the disciples because it signaled that Jesus's Way had been vindicated by God—especially that most difficult bit about dying for the cause rather than killing for the cause.

This vocabulary suggests that the disciples were caught between two types of fear: the terror produced by the state, particularly in times of war, and the awe that comes in the presence of Divine Power. How contemporary sounding is this dilemma in our world, riddled with terrorism both official and ad hoc. It poses a revealing question to us, sharpened intensely by this last Iraq war. Who generates "shock and awe" in our lives? Is it the Pentagon's power of death over life or the biblical God's power of life over death? This is the preeminent theological question of our time.

The Prophetic Vocation of "Connecting the Dots"

The last scene, in counterpoint, is almost whimsical, as Jesus tries to convince his friends that he's not a ghost, having already gone unrecognized once (24:38-39). Tired, he asks, in effect: "Man, these have been a long couple of days and I've been through a lot; does anyone have a sandwich for a brother?" (24:41). Then, after breaking the fast he declared at the Last Supper (Luke 22:16–19), Jesus resumes the Bible study he began on the road to Emmaus: "And he said to them, 'These are the words which I spoke to you, while I was with you: that all things must be fulfilled, which were written in the law of Moses, and the prophets, and the psalms, concerning me'" (24:44).

The following verse reads: "Then he opened their minds, so that they might understand the scriptures" (24:45). These two verbs used here tell an interesting story. Again (as in verse 32) we encounter *dianoigo*, to open faculties of perception that have been shut down by empire. The verb "to understand" (Greek, *suniemi*) is an unusual one, meaning to bring together all the data; I would paraphrase it as "connecting the dots." In the New Testament it is usually employed to describe those many situations in which disciples are *unable* to make such connections (e.g., Luke 2:50, 18:34; Acts 7:25).

Both verbs are specifically connected in the gospels with the story of the call of Isaiah (Isaiah 6:1ff; see Luke 8:10; Acts 28:26-27). Jesus is thus reminding his followers of something the prophets long ago stipulated: people will oppose the Word of God because it challenges us to *change*. And what we resist most fiercely is, again, that terrible truth: "It is *inevitable* that Messiah should suffer at the hands of the leaders" (24:46). Because this prophetic vocation (and fate) is one disciples are now invited to share: "Repentance and forgiveness of sins should be preached in his name to all nations, beginning from Jerusalem. You are witnesses [Greek, *martures*] of these things" (24:47-48). Everyone in America may want to be a millionaire, but no one wants to be a martyr.

Here, then, is what we learn from the Emmaus road story:

1. The resurrected Jesus appears first as a Stranger—indeed, as one needing hospitality. Let this be a Christological lesson to the church!

2. Rather than standing idly among peaceable religious folk who are insulated and aloof from the world, this Risen Christ is moving alongside disciples who are in trouble because they have sought to change it.

3. Jesus is pastoral, seeking to know the pain of those struggling with a specifically political context, rather than offering saccharine spiritual assurances of personal immunity from historical consequences.

4. Yet he is also prophetic, his biblical analysis centered around a fierce prophetic hermeneutic in order to reframe the empire's historiography with the alternative story of transformation from the margins.

How desperately we U.S. Christians need *this* Jesus to walk with us under our present imperial Shadow of Death! And how urgent it is that we reread our Bibles and our history through the lens of the *prophets*.

Today, social conservatives and political oligarchs have hijacked the Bible in public discourse in the United States. But let us not think we are bereft of practitioners of this Emmaus road kind of theological reflection. Dietrich Bonhoeffer's Finkenwald seminary mounted resistance to the Nazi Reich, and his profound *Letters and Papers from Prison* survived his execution. Dorothy Day's reflections on serving the poor in the context of the Catholic Worker movement remind us of the "long loneliness" of solidarity. Exiled Guatemalan poet Julia Esquivel's defiant tomes birthed hope in the midst of her country's genocide. Philip Berrigan's persistent nonviolent witness against the arms race over four decades never let us forget that we live under the Shadow of Nuclear Death.

But it was Martin Luther King, Jr., who best exemplified the task of doing theology on the run. In particular in this time of war we ought to revisit his prophetic "Beyond Vietnam" speech, given on April 4, 1967, at Riverside Church, exactly a year, almost to the hour, before he was gunned down in Memphis. For this speech is a magnificent example of "connecting the dots" between the three great pathologies of American imperial culture: racism, militarism, and poverty.[5] King "and all the other prophets" can help us reread our own national history.

W. A. Williams concluded his own great study of this history with a pressing query which is, I believe, ultimately theological: "Do we have either the imagination or the courage to say 'no' to empire? It is now our responsibility. It has to do with how we live and how we die. We as a culture have run out of imperial games to play."[6] May the North American church rediscover courage and character enough to engage this question, buoyed by an Easter faith and tutored by the prophetic tradition.

Notes

1. William Appleman Williams, *Empire as a Way of Life* (New York: Oxford University Press, 1980), viii.

2. Ibid., 13.

3. Posted at www.alternet.org/waroniraq/21780/ on April 18, 2005.

4. See my *Binding the Strong Man: A Political Reading of Mark's Story of Jesus* (Maryknoll, N.Y.: Orbis, 1988), 358ff.

5. The text and an audio excerpt of this speech can be found at www.drmartinlutherkingjr.com/beyondvietnam.htm.

6. Williams, *Empire as a Way of Life.*

A Christian Response to Mass Incarceration: Unbind Them!

VIVIAN DENISE NIXON

And [s]he who had died came out bound hand and foot with grave clothes, and [her] face was wrapped with a cloth. Jesus said to them, "Loose [her], and let [her] go."

—*John 11:44*

I arose from my tomblike cell on the morning of March 19, 2001, in response to a commanding shout: "Nixon—pack up!" The time had come; the stone was rolled away. Free to leave, I suppressed flutters of joy and panic. Joy because I had survived. Panic because I would enter a world that now opined, "By now [s]he stinketh" (John 11:39). Survival is the most I had hoped for in the early days. I would have settled for an invisible existence in a place where no one recognized my disgrace. To my dismay, I discovered that it is not likely, in American society, for one to live down the deadly stench of criminal conviction and incarceration. Hindered by restrictive legal statutes, stereotypical public perceptions, and stigma reinforced by self-righteous religiosity, I was bound. My hands were bound: I could not reach for the stars. My feet were bound: I could not walk into my destiny. My face was covered: My tears could not be seen.

Blessed with a strong understanding of the liberating message of the gospel, I soon rejected the idea of becoming one of the walking dead. Believing that Christ saves by grace and not *dis*grace, I chose to turn my biggest mess into my greatest miracle. I prepared myself by getting educated and gaining an intimate knowledge of how criminal justice systems and policies control the lives of people of color in poor urban communities. Most important, I abandoned the fear of embarrassment and public exposure that would almost certainly be a consequence of the work that I now do—work that is slowly unraveling the grave clothes that bind me and millions of others who are trying to rebuild their lives.

Even with divinely endowed courage, it is patently unnerving for me to walk down the corridors of any prison after having lived in a medium-security prison for nearly four years. I am not afraid of the men or women in orange, green, or brown jumpsuits, nor am I unduly leery of the gray-clad officials. Rather, I am harassed by an invisible presence—the public spirit of punishment and dehumanization that has become, as T. Richard Snyder observes in *The Protestant Ethic and the Spirit of Punishment*, "part of the air we breathe."

Punishment and retribution have become such a normal part of the way we do justice in the United States that Christians and non-Christians alike hardly acknowledge the peril of inhaling the systemic smog in which written codes of law treat men and women as if upon being accused of a crime they cease to be persons and become things. We have so dehumanized people that it has become acceptable to allocate more than $50 billion annually to exile and penalize them. Two decades of "tough on crime" and "war on drugs" political rhetoric has driven the electorate to support policies that include mandatory minimum sentences (which nullify judicial discretion), far-reaching prosecutorial power, adult prosecution of juveniles, the elimination of parole, public humiliation of selected defendants, and reinstitution of the death penalty in numerous states. More explicitly, in 1976 California struck the word *rehabilitation* from its criminal code and passed a law stating, "The purpose of imprisonment is punishment."

According to Bureau of Justice Statistics, over the past twenty-five years the U.S. incarceration rate has more than quadrupled. That rate —723 prisoners for every 100,000 people—is the highest in the industrialized world. With just over 5 percent of the world's population, the United States now holds 24 percent of the world's prisoners. Terms like "mass incarceration," "prison industrial complex," and "collateral consequences of conviction" were invented to describe the ironies and disquieting sociological contortions of this period. Or we can put it more concretely: for millions of individuals and their families, prison has become the primary means for dealing with difficult social problems such as homelessness, drug abuse, mental illness, illiteracy, and poverty. On the other side of the fence are those American citizens hypnotized by the sensationalized version of crime and justice depicted in the media and caught in a cycle of misperceptions of—and reactive responses to—mass incarceration. People do not know whether to perceive crime as a pubic safety issue, a social issue, a political issue, a moral issue, an economic issue, or a spiritual issue.

One thing is clear after thirty years: legislators, law enforcers, and corrections administrators have figured out that warehousing millions of Americans in prisons is no longer *economically* sustainable. This partly explains the turn toward prison privatization schemes, which absolved governments of the responsibility for the daily care of people held in private prisons. But privatization did *not* reduce costs; it only reduced services, and after numerous scandals, escapes, and horrendous incidents of abuse against incarcerated people—including many deaths—the allure of privatization has lately been fading.

Today policing and corrections experts, policy makers, reformers, advocates, activist nonprofit organizations, and faith-based organizations are each taking their best shot at coming up with viable solutions. For most groups seeking to do this work, however, a *viable* solution must translate into a *fundable* solution, which means that root causes are still not addressed. Afraid to appear soft on crime and unwilling to admit that the hegemony of privilege is responsible for existing social conditions, including mass incarceration, most mainstream, well-funded groups working on policing, corrections, and community-based solutions to mass incarceration try only to stop the *growth* of prison populations, without troubling themselves with the root causes of this systemic disaster.

In his 2004 State of the Union address, President George W. Bush asked the Congress to take steps to empower religious institutions, through the White House Office of Faith-Based and Community Initiatives, to give former prisoners a "second chance" by helping them find work, homes, and faith-based mentors. The Christian helping strategy, as it pertains to prisons and the people who live in them, has traditionally focused on individual transformation. Prison ministries of all faiths, but particularly those that embrace Christian traditions, tend to link an imprisoned person's success or failure largely to the individual's confession of repentance, salvation, and subsequent moral behavior. Policy makers and nonprofit organizations purporting to endorse rehabilitative approaches to criminal justice also focus on the convicted individual's need to change his or her behavior. This is such a prevalent theme in rehabilitation programs that people who are in treatment often construct self-castigating inner monologues that later become theater for counselors, corrections personnel, parole personnel, clergy, and others who will at some point judge the individual worthy, or not worthy, of a "second chance." Such strategies, however, offer temporary solutions but do not assure long-term success. They also partake of the same dehumanizing currents that created mass incarceration to begin with.

People who experience criminal conviction and incarceration often describe confinement to the prison house as a type of death. In the same way, the emergence from prison back to outside life is associated with resurrection. The typical prison resurrection narrative, often applauded by prison chaplains and visiting prison ministries, is replete with criticism and denunciation of one's former self, acknowledgment of guilt and shame, and claims of absolute transformation. During an unprecedented one-day symposium at Pennsylvania's Graterford State Prison, a group of incarcerated men who have developed a theory they refer to as "the culture of street crime" invoked the rhetoric of death and resurrection repeatedly. During one portion of the presentation, a young black man living at Graterford performed a rap monologue during which the refrain "It's all my fault!" was repeated no fewer than fifteen times. No one cringed. No one acknowledged his pain and courage. No one apologized to him for a society in which the cumulative denial of human rights has emasculated eight generations of black men and that now expects them to perform social compliance as if unaffected by their ancestral trauma. No one jumped up and rescued him by saying, "No, son, it really isn't *all* your fault."

This is not to say that personal accountably is a nonfactor. To be answerable to one's self from a psychological perspective—and to one's God from a spiritual perspective—promotes healing and liberates one from a kind of deep-seated shame that can never produce change. But the degree to which an individual is socially accountable cannot exceed the degree to which society has been accountable to that individual. The accountability approach falls short when we acknowledge that the stake in social norms is different for a disadvantaged minority person who exists as a frustrated outsider on the fringes of dominant socioeconomic structure: unemployed, inadequately educated, living in substandard housing, lacking health care, enduring police harassment, and excluded from the political process. As W. E. B. DuBois noted in *The Souls of Black Folk*, "the Negro is coming more and more to look upon law and justice, not as protecting safeguards, but as sources of humiliation and oppression. The laws are made by men who have little interest in him; they are executed by men who have absolutely no motive for treating the black people with courtesy or consideration; and, finally, the accused law-breaker is tried, not by his peers, but too often by men who would rather punish ten innocent Negroes than let one guilty one escape." An adequate understanding of the state of criminal justice in America must begin with the acknowledgement that this perception of law still prevails in large sections of the minority community.

In varying degrees of contrast to the individual transformation/individual accountability approach (to evangelicals, the soul-saving approach), the prison reformers and activists whom conservatives brand as radical leftists tend to focus on the need for *systemic* change. Many call for the complete abolition of the criminal justice system as it now exists. This would include a nationwide moratorium on prison construction and the death penalty, less intrusive policing, less prosecutorial authority, abolition of mandatory minimum sentences, a constitutional amendment restoring voting rights to all prisoners and former prisoners, and the elimination of all laws that restrict postincarceration rights and privileges. Some would go so far as to recommend that putting people in cages is not acceptable under any circumstances.

The sides are now deeply entrenched in the debate over whether to utilize in-prison programs and community-based alternatives to promote personal accountability or whether to change laws and polices that send people to prison in the first place. It is certainly easier to convince a largely Christian public that an incarcerated person is worthy of a "second chance" if that person appears to be penitent and in some way converted. And there is nothing inherently invalid about repentance as a private spiritual exercise. There is, however, grave danger in promoting the perception that all people who are sent to prison are evil, sinful people, and that leading them to Jesus (or any other route to personal transformation) is the answer to all that is wrong with the criminal justice system. It is also dangerous, in a more enduring sense, to believe that we can "fix" the multitude of social evils that now present themselves as criminal justice issues by simply changing a few laws and creating more government and community programs.

Emotion-laden tirades such as the following, which was part of a campaign ad run by Ronald Reagan in 1980 in support of an all-out "war on drugs," give reason to believe that there is an evil within the hysteria that drives mass incarceration:

> Every day the jungle draws a little closer. Our city streets are jungle paths after dark.... Man's determination to live under the protection of the law has pushed back the jungle down through the centuries. But the jungle is always there, and somehow it seems much closer than we have known it in the years preceding. With all our science and sophistication... the jungle still is waiting to take over. The man with the badge holds it back.

One need only look at the race dynamics of the arrest, prosecution, and sentencing processes to understand the correlation between the racism of this campaign ad and the targeting of certain communities (jungles) for surveillance and incarceration.

The United States imprisons more black men and women per capita than the apartheid regime of South Africa ever did. Of the 2.1 million men and women in U.S. jails and prisons at the end of 2003, 44 percent were African Americans, though African Americans comprised only 12.3 percent of the U.S. population. Black males have a 32 percent chance of serving time in prison at some point in their lives; Hispanic males have a 17 percent chance; white males have a 6 percent chance. Low-income women of color are the fastest-growing prison demographic. One reason for this disparity is the drug laws designed to punish with mandatory prison terms those who possess crack cocaine (used in the black community), while penalties for possession of the powder form (used by middle- and upper-class whites) usually take the form of monetary fines and do not include mandatory prison sentences. If the white drug-using and drug-selling population were targeted as relentlessly and prosecuted as vigorously as minority populations, there would be anarchy in the streets.

Why would a supposedly moral and largely Christian society design a criminal justice system with such a disparate impact unless there are evil forces at work? Evil spirits are not restricted to the hearts and minds of incarcerated men and women: they live and move among principalities and powers—among the rulers of the darkness of this age, to use Paul's language.

In addition to the sharply racialized profile of Americans who are in prison, there are invisible punishments and collateral consequences that continue to punish people after they are released from prison. These collateral consequences punish the families of people with criminal convictions and penalize entire poor communities of color, whose residents are disproportionately represented in the prison population. Research by Susan Tucker and Eric Cadora in New York, reported in *Ideas for an Open Society: Justice Reinvestment,* shows that a "million dollars a year is used to incarcerate people from one block in Brooklyn—over half for non-violent drug offenses—and return them, on average, in less than three years stigmatized, unskilled, and untrained to the same unchanged block." This is happening in low-income neighborhoods across the country. There are not enough resources in the community to support the successful reintegration of the men and women who return to these neighborhoods after having been imprisoned for extended periods of time. The community, which has been destabilized by the removal of large numbers of citizens who previously contributed to its social fabric and economic structure, becomes further disadvantaged by its inability to respond to the needs of formerly incarcerated people who are their neighbors and family members. Hundreds of changes to state and federal laws impose additional penalties on people with felony convictions. These laws include electoral disenfranchisement and limited access to education, public housing, health care, and certain trades and professions. Facing civic death, poor employment prospects, homelessness, and social stigma, many people released from prison are reincarcerated within three years (most due to minor parole violations such as missed curfews, missed appointments, or failed drug tests). This cycle of imprisonment does nothing to increase public safety; in fact, these communities have reached a criminal justice "tipping point"—the juncture at which repressive state policies that cause mass incarceration incapacitate neighborhood social networks to the point where people are less safe.

Christians of all persuasions seem to know that they ought to be involved in confronting the disparities in the criminal justice system or (at the very least) ministering to the people most affected by it. As Harmon Wray notes in "Models of Criminal Justice Ministry and Resistance," "upper-middle class predominantly white mainstream denominations pass enlightened and progressive resolutions on criminal justice issues, which largely go unpreached and untaught; fundamentalist, and Pentecostal-holiness groups do hands-on jail and prison ministry, usually as volunteers, focusing on [saving] individual prisoners." In the midst of this, the prophetic voice of Jehovah Tsidkenu (God of Justice), who calls us "to do justly, to love kindness and to walk humbly" in his presence (Micah 6:6–8), is clearly absent. A life of Christian principles and righteous influence requires more than the imposition of a fundamentalist morality; it requires a commitment to social justice. It requires interaction with the divine and interaction with society, each relationship enlightening and shaping the other.

Since the Christian church as an institution is well established in the marketplace and is practically part of the functioning of the government and the economy, it is unlikely that it will become an oppositional force at the upper levels. Individual Christians, however, can choose to use Jesus's example of social justice to distinguish their own activities and positions from those of the institutional church. To act on behalf of the oppressed *may* or may *not* indicate that an individual is a follower of Jesus Christ. Conversely, as Robert McAfee Brown often said, "the sign of *not* knowing God is to do injustice." Christian pundits talk about justice but stop short of confronting the powers and principalities that create injustice. This is largely because religion and government are politically intertwined. Politicians say what Christians want to hear in order to win votes, and Christians respond favorably in hopes of gaining lucrative government contracts to do prison ministry. One such example is Chuck Colson's Prison Fellowship, which has been granted millions of state and federal dollars for faith-based work in and out of prisons. As governor of Texas, George W. Bush awarded Colson a contract to establish InnerChange Freedom Initiative, a Bible-centered fundamentalist prison-within-a-prison. Now that Mr. Bush is president, there is the potential for many more "Christian" prisons to emerge under the control of conservative groups like Prison Fellowship, which has become a large national organization.

It is expected and hoped that a Christian's understanding of the gospel will inform all that he or she does, including the forming of opinions on political and social issues. But this becomes unlikely when the masses of those who profess the Christian faith get their biblical instruction from fundamentalist leaders who support systems and policies that defy the basic spiritual and ethical principles of justice, peace, equality, freedom, reconciliation, and forgiveness that are the actual teachings of Christ. These leaders are seen as worthy of a following because they have aligned themselves, quite visibly, with the prevailing establishment. For their part, the followers seem unaware that there is no precedent of Jesus joining forces with the rulers and kings of his day. Jesus was with the prostitutes, the tax collectors, and the lepers. Other Christians, though perhaps not subject to fundamentalist messages, are tied to mainstream congregations that limit their outreach strategies to the well-intentioned but disempowering ministries of feeding and fixing people. An authentic walk with God, however, moves human beings away from structural power and away from paternalistic benevolence and into the realm of spiritual power found in dialogue with God. In that discourse, seekers will find personal truth and with it the fortitude to stand firm in that truth before opposing forces.

James Cone suggests in A *Black Theology of Liberation* that "authentic love is not 'help'—not giving Christmas baskets—but working for political, social, and economic justice, which always means a redistribution of power. It is the kind of power which enables [the oppressed] to fight their own battles and thus keep their dignity." Christians who choose to become agents of social change cannot do so effectively by focusing solely on the salvation of individuals. Would-be reformers must change their spiritual lens from one of evangelizing to one of social justice. In practice that could certainly *begin* with visiting prisons and establishing genuine reciprocal relationships with people who live there. But those relationships ought to eventually instill the incarcerated person with a sense of personal power. Christians who share their faith with incarcerated or formerly incarcerated people can be effective by telling their own stories, revealing their own inadequacies, and showing how faith makes a difference in their lives—not by preaching to prison residents about how they need to change. For Christians, visiting prisoners is hypocritical if nonproselytizing compassion is not also extended to Muslims, Hindus, Jews, Buddhists, atheists, LGBT prisoners, and all behind the walls who do not consider themselves "unsaved" but who still want and need companionship and (in many cases) mentors.

Prison ministries that do not also address systemic problems have nonetheless provided real solutions for some people. The changes made in those lives are precious and remind us that the Good Shepherd never abandons the one lost sheep. However, we must remember that the primary legacy that Jesus left was empowerment. He promised the disciples that they would receive power from on high and that they would do greater works than Christ himself did. Moving beyond the evangelizing model and into a social justice model requires a transfer of power to the powerless that transforms their lives in one or more of the following ways: they recognize power that they already have, they recover power that they once had and lost, or they receive power that they never had before. Richard Couto talks about two key types of empowerment in "Community Coalitions and Grassroots Policies of Empowerment." The first—psychopolitical empowerment—increases a person's self-esteem and changes the allocation of resources and/or the actions of others. In other words, psychopolitical empowerment involves the confidence, desire, and ability of the formerly powerless to bring about real change. The second form of empowerment—psychosymbolic empowerment—raises a person's ability to survive in an unchanged set of circumstances. What oppressed people need most is the first kind of empowerment. More often than not, even the most forward-thinking policies and programs deliver the second kind.

Aware that each year nearly 630,000 people leave America's prisons and return to their communities, America is in the midst of what Glen Martin of the Legal Action Center's H.I.R.E. Network calls *reentry mania*. Various reform models are being peddled around the country in anticipation of the federal government's promise to legitimize and assist faith-based and community-based programs that support the successful transitions of people from prison into the community. Strategies run the gamut from Christian programs in and out of prisons claiming to eliminate criminal behavior by saving souls to calls for less surveillance, less imprisonment, fair and alternative sentencing, more treatment (instead of criminalization) of behaviors related to addiction and mental illness, and less use of media to hypnotize the public into a state of hypervigilance by relentlessly retelling every gory crime. Reentry expert Jeremy Travis recommends community-based reentry courts; Travis has even written an expansive reentry manual suggesting "five principles for successful reentry and five building blocks for a new jurisprudence of prisoner reintegration. The government-sponsored Re-entry Policy Council recently released a report containing seven hundred pages of recommendations for policy and best practices in reentry. Some ideas have already begun to take hold.

Restorative justice models are popular in all camps. Conservatives, liberals, Christian evangelicals, and secular reformists have come together in an unlikely alliance to support programs that hold people who are accused of crimes accountable—shaming and punishing them in a *gentler* way—while allowing victims the opportunity to confront the person who has caused them harm as well to receive some type of restitution. Thus, in theory, restoration occurs and the dangers of overpunishing are avoided. But legal experts Brenda Sims Blackwell and Clark D. Cunningham remind us in "Taking the Punishment out of the Process" that restorative justice works best when it is certain that a crime has been committed, that the "offender" has been irrefutably identified, and that the person is being prosecuted in response to a complaint by a victim or victims and not by a regulatory state.

Justice reinvestment is another idea that has some potential to heal the communities that have been most damaged by existing criminal justice policy and practice. Broadly, justice reinvestment means reevaluating social and political priorities. It proposes that some portion of the billions of dollars America now spends on prisons should be used to provide resources to the communities that have been most affected by the overuse of incarceration. Building better schools, health care facilities, parks, and public spaces supplies neighborhoods with the infrastructure needed to support the burden of accountability they bear for the successful transition of people from prison to the community.

Employment-based reentry models are popular in government and policy circles because they typically have the specific goal of putting large numbers of formerly incarcerated people to work in a short period of time, which makes for good data. But participants typically end up in minimum wage jobs, which fail to lift them out of poverty and thus ensure their continued marginality.

Investment in higher education has been the *least* explored solution, even though it has proven most effective time and time again. Various studies have shown that college education reduces the recidivism rate from 66 percent down to as low as 7.7 percent. Upon completing a three-year process evaluation of the College and Community Fellowship (a groundbreaking college-based reentry program at The City University of New York), Michelle Ronda and Will Weikart were able to report a recidivism rate of zero.

The long-term benefits of higher education for the student are many. Over an adult's working life, bachelor's degree holders earn about twice as much as those with only a high school diploma. But there are better reasons for investing in education-based reentry programs. Aside from increased lifetime earning potential, people who attain higher education acquire an intimate knowledge of the systems and policies that control their lives along with a political and social consciousness that gives them a type of power that they did not have before. Education, then, initiates a true shift of power, in that the educated person gets hold of knowledge that expands his or her capacity to resist an oppressive regime rather than succumb for lack of options. All the policing and all the prisons in the world are not as good at ensuring a free and functioning civil society as is serious investment in education. Yet in 1994 the federal government decided to ban incarcerated people from receiving Pell grants. The government did this despite studies by the Justice Policy Institute, among others, demonstrating that the more education a person has, the less likely he or she is to return to prison *and* despite the fact that payment to educators on behalf of imprisoned students amounted to less then *one-tenth of 1 percent* of total Pell expenditures. Adding to this madness, the 1998 reauthorization of the Higher Education Act renders reentering men and women with drug convictions ineligible for the kinds of student aid available to other students.

So proposed solutions are plentiful. But with the exception of investment in higher education, all of the reform strategies now under discussion tend to attack symptoms rather than causes. They exemplify Couto's model of psychosymbolic empowerment by raising the ability of the oppressed to survive in an unchanged set of circumstances. Initiating these programs may provide some immediate relief to the battle-weary casualties of the drug war, and it may ease the conscience of the reformers, but in truth, not much will change. If employment programs prevail, more people will work. If community-based reentry courts and restorative justice schemes succeed, there will be reconciliations that bring some people together. If mandatory minimums are outlawed, fewer people will go to prison and those who go may serve shorter sentences. If justice reinvestment takes hold, some communities will have their parks, schools, and community centers restored. Yet even if *all* of these worthy goals are accomplished, they will happen under the banner of an unchanged social construction that relegates dark-skinned people to a permanent underclass. Even if fewer people are going to prison, those who *do* go will continue to be disproportionately representative of poor people and people of color.

Paradigms that call for radical change (change that shifts the balance of power at the *radix*, or root, of things) rarely gain credence or support from the structures that are most threatened by them. Theologian Robert McAfee Brown notes that it is one thing to acknowledge *intellectually* that if a system based on punishment and retribution applied disproportionately to poor people and people of color only subjugates and destroys, then the system must go; but it is a different thing altogether for those who argue that the system should go to be prepared to surrender their *own* power, their own status, their luxuries, their advantage. Yet this level of discipleship is what will be required to break the back of a system that oppresses so many on so many levels.

The challenge to Christians, and to all people who are serious about their desire to live in an open and just society, is to return to the radical understanding of social justice that was present in earlier outbursts of progressive and religious social and political reform in the United States and abroad. The antiwar movements, labor movements, civil rights movements, and human rights movements that preceded today's prison reform movement all sought—and still seek—to model the radical nature of Jesus's mortal ministry in that they do not flinch at the opportunity to lift up the oppressed and hold the oppressor accountable, nor do they hesitate to speak truth to power. Our efforts to eradicate the prison industrial complex, to provide better opportunities for people affected by criminal conviction, and to repair the breach in communities that have been devastated by systematic criminalization can only be successful if they are linked to the deeper and broader movement for social transformation.

Naming the evil as racism is never an easy thing. It is hard for whites to think in these terms because for the most part they see racism as something outside of themselves. Either they are liberal and feel far removed from it, or they are conservative and feel that racism is in America's past and that black people should simply "get over it." Grounded in American opportunity myths, conservative racism blames black Americans for their own failure to live up to white standards in a supposedly now colorblind society. Liberal racism is closeted and private because liberals are so uncomfortable with it that they deny it exists. They tend to throw services and programs at the surface-level problem. But as Cornel West wrote in *Race Matters*, "To engage in a serious discussion of race in America, we must begin not with the problems of Black people but with the flaws of American society—flaws rooted in historic inequalities and longstanding cultural stereotypes. How we set up the terms for discussing racial issues shapes our perception and response to these issues. As long as Black people are viewed as a 'them,' the burden falls on Blacks to do all the 'cultural' and 'moral' work necessary for healthy race relations. The implication is that only certain Americans can define what it means to be American—and the rest must simply 'fit in.'"

Thus, even as we work to end the scandal of mass incarceration and the criminalization of communities of color, it is not *just* the criminal justice system as such that we wrestle with on a spiritual level. We struggle with the evil of racism as well. We struggle with it not as some disembodied demonic being but as a *social invention* that has assumed demonic characteristics. Rooted deeply in our history and institutions, racism has taken on a life of its own. It has become self-perpetuating, self-justifying, and deceptively predatory. If the immense gap between races in America is ever to be bridged, it will require a dialogue in which people are prepared to face their own demons, to fully understand how they benefit from a racist system, to voice more than noble intent and pious ideologies, and to acknowledge the multigenerational suffering of African American people.

The body of Lazarus was alive but not free as long as he remained bound with the limitations that were put on him by those who declared him dead. Even if the call "Lazarus come forth!" echoes through every prison and every jail throughout the nation, and even if all the prison gates fly open, the work will not be complete. Years of struggle will lie before us as we follow Christ's command to unbind the hands and feet and faces of the newly resurrected souls: to remove the limitations that were imposed on the dead by the living, to peel away the layers of racism, classism, sexism, and social dominance that bound them and sent them to their deaths.

Approaching social problems from the root can be overwhelming because there are no prescriptive answers, only endless struggle. But in faith and through faith, Christians can find a peculiar hope in struggle. We understand that involvement in the greater divine plan is not about results but about process—about exploring the infinite possibilities of the human spirit. Cornel West calls this "combative spiritually." It is, he says, the kind of spiritual warfare that "accents political struggle but goes beyond it by looking death, and dread, and despair, and disappointment, and disease in the face and saying there is, in fact, hope beyond these."

The craving our culture has for overnight solutions works against hope, because hope is for the long-distance runner. By faith we enter the struggle not because we need an immediate win but because the cause is right. In the end, each of us is measured by how and why we engage the struggle. We are the ones who will account to our consciences for the choices we make.

Who Is My Neighbor? Reflections on Our Changing Neighborhood in the Global Economy

RICK UFFORD-CHASE

You shall love your neighbor as yourself.

—*Matthew* 22:39

There is nothing particularly remarkable about Sagrada Familia (Holy Family) Parish. It's located in the small, dusty city of Agua Prieta, Sonora, just across the border from Douglas, Arizona. Six blocks south from the port of entry at the U.S.-Mexico border and a few blocks to the west, one crosses to the wrong side of the railroad tracks. This is a neighborhood of rutted dirt roads and small adobe houses, many of which long ago fell into disrepair. Still, watered flowers in dirt front yards are evidence of hopeful inhabitants who have raised their families here. The church has a modern, 1960s-style bell tower that can be seen and heard from all over the neighborhood. Though it reaches into the sky, it functions more as an anchor for a neighborhood whose legacy is to have been planted on the wrong side of town.

Two things keep this area of twelve square blocks from total despair. One is the stubborn rootedness of the families who moved here from southern Mexico beginning forty years ago. Even as petty crime, assault, and drug smuggling have become an inescapable fact of life, these men and women have refused to move out. This is where they raised their children, and they remain even after many of their children have moved across town or crossed the border to head north to Tucson and Phoenix.

The other refusal to give in to despair is the presence of the church itself. This church has lived through good times and bad times, through priests who committed to this difficult place in which to do ministry, and through others who appeared to care not one whit for the people of

God who surround the church. The church has been a rock, supporting many of the women when their husbands headed north to find work years ago, and has functioned as the center of community life.

Agua Prieta exists on the border between the "first world" of the developed North and the "two-thirds world" of poverty and economic marginalization in the Global South. This border is perhaps the most important place one could go in the Western Hemisphere to consider the question "Who is my neighbor?"

Most of us in the United States have completely embraced a worldview that most Mexicans know is based on a lie—that it is acceptable for those of us who had the good fortune to be born on the U.S. side of the border to receive all of the benefits of the global economy while taking no responsibility for the global community. Naming and standing against that lie is one of the defining challenges for the church in the United States in our time. But to name one must see, and looking at this poor church in a poor neighborhood on the wrong side of the tracks and the wrong side of the border is an ideal place to start.

Most of the women who are raising kids in Agua Prieta aren't from here. They came north sometime over the last twenty to thirty years as it became obvious that there was nothing left for them in their rural communities. Thirty years ago in Mexico, roughly 75 percent of the population was rural. Today, most folks have fled the dead-end poverty of an agricultural economy that has been largely abandoned for the glitter and promise of the industrial export-led economy. In the countryside, it has become almost impossible to find a job, even one that pays just $2 a day. If you are lucky enough to own your own land, you're not much better off. Only an urban observer could romanticize the despair of trying to compete as a small farmer in the global economy. As a result, cities in the urbanized border region have ballooned along with the shift in population; today, 75 percent of the population of Mexico is urban.

What are the forces at play underneath that rural to urban shift?

Mexico, and most of the rest of Latin America as well, could reasonably be described as a "single-export economy" through the first seventy years of the last century. Mexicans lived a subsistence lifestyle. The few foreign dollars that did arrive came from a few basic items for export that were extracted from—or grown on—the land. Although most Mexicans had little money, they were able to provide the basics for their families through growing food or bartering with one another. In the 1960s, Mexico's economy was growing steadily, with 6 or 7 percent growth in its gross domestic product year after year. In fact, many economists referred to the decade as the "Mexican Miracle."

During those years, Mexico's government looked toward the United States as the best example of an economy that had successfully made the shift from dependence on one or a few exports to one of self-sufficiency, in which it could produce most of its citizens' basic needs. Slowly at first, both the government and Mexican businesspeople began to seek financing for development from foreign "for-profit" banking institutions. The rate of borrowing accelerated dramatically after the oil crisis of the early 1970s, as banking institutions in the North went looking for clients to take loans from their burgeoning reserves of petrodollars.

The history invites an obvious question: How did Mexico go from a growing economy with low-interest loans to a debt crisis of unimaginable proportions?

The answer is complex but can be summarized. Some of the money went into attempts to build legitimate businesses created to help the country substitute its own production for items previously imported, and many of those businesses failed. Some money disappeared into other projects where corruption was rampant or where the business plans were ill conceived. Much of the money disappeared through capital flight as Mexican investors took their dollars outside the country instead of reinvesting in their own economy.

The most important dynamic, however, was the fact that the rates of interest on the loans were pegged to the prime rate set by the Federal Reserve in the United States. In 1979 rates rose from 5 or 6 percent to almost 20 percent interest as the Fed sought to stem rising inflation in the

United States. This was a circumstance far beyond Mexico's control, but Mexicans' loan payments skyrocketed as unpaid interest was added to the original principal in the early 1980s.

Enter the International Monetary Fund (IMF). In an attempt to bring "discipline" to economies in trouble and help them manage their debt payments, the IMF instituted severe economic measures in countries all over the world that shared Mexico's woes. Those measures were called Structural Adjustment Programs, and whatever their intent may have been, one of their effects was to accelerate the rural to urban shift experienced by the folks at Sagrada Familia Catholic Church in Agua Prieta.

The idea was simple. In the IMF's view Mexico needed to move government subsidies away from the agricultural and small-farm sector and build up the industrial sector, which would attract foreign dollars to pay the debt. One older man I know explained it better than anyone else I've met. He owned his own small farm in a fertile coastal plain in Sinaloa, the state just to the south of the border state of Sonora. In the mid-1980s, he experienced two years of drought in a row. It was not that he had never experienced bad crop cycles before. But this time when he went to a government bank for small farmers, he discovered they had no more money to loan. Instead of the government-backed loan at 7 percent interest he had received in the past, his only option was to risk a loan from one of the predatory lenders who charged almost 35 percent interest per year. Within a year, his two oldest teenagers had come north to find work, and within another year, the rest of the family had followed them.

This, of course, was exactly the intended consequence. If Mexico was to attract U.S. corporations to set up factories and bring in the dollars needed to pay the debt, it needed to prepare workers for the global assembly line, not for the farm. Cities like Agua Prieta boomed; most have grown by more than a factor of ten in fewer than twenty-five years.

This takes us back to those women at the church. What happened to them as they tried to make a life for themselves in this new and foreign place?

Life on the economic margins of every industrial city in Latin America is hard, and the border is no different. As recent arrivals to Agua Prieta went to work in the factories, they discovered that they had jumped from the frying pan into the fire. At first, a secure paycheck seemed like a genuine move toward economic security after the vagaries of life on the farm. As consumers, however, they were no longer able to grow their own food or barter in the local market. Now they shopped in the supermarkets and department stores of the global economy.

One friend of mine has raised three boys to young adulthood in Agua Prieta. Now that they are older teenagers; they've dropped out of school and gone to work in factories to help support the family. For years their mother worked a sixty-hour week and took home a paycheck of $50 to $60. When she shopped for their groceries each week, she discovered that a gallon of milk cost more than $3. Put more viscerally, she had to work more than three hours to buy a gallon of milk. Most other items were similarly high priced. Eventually she was able to get a border-crossing card that allowed her to visit Douglas, Arizona. There, she discovered that it was far cheaper to do her grocery shopping at the Safeway on the U.S. side of the border than it was to shop in Agua Prieta. The situation remains the same today. The only difference is that there are now four wage earners helping her family to survive instead of one, though they continue to live in housing that would be considered substandard in any community in the United States.

This family, like so many others I've known, offers a living example of the irony of the global economy. Even as Mexico can now claim to be healthy at the macroeconomic level—that is, to continue to make its debt payments—Mexicans today are poorer than at any other time in Mexico's history. They are working in factories making seat belts, cellular telephones, women's underwear, computer boards, surgical prep kits, and the like. While they work at a tenth of our wages to provide the most basic goods we in the United States depend upon, they must purchase these same goods at roughly the same prices we pay in the developed North. A few years ago I knew a woman who made household extension cords for GE, then crossed the border to shop in a Wal-Mart where she bought those same extension cords to take home and plug in her few appliances.

In the end, our Latin American brothers and sisters present us with the most theologically challenging question of our time: "Who is my neighbor?" And the answer, perhaps more obvious here on the border than anywhere else in the world, is that relationships between neighbors cannot be limited by nation-state borders, or even by our inability to know one another personally. Our neighborhood crosses *all* borders, and our neighbor is now everyone, everywhere.

In fact, Jesus suggested the same two thousand years ago.

> Just then a lawyer stood up to test Jesus. "Teacher," he said, "what must I do to inherit eternal life?" He said to him, "What is written in the law? What do you read there?" He answered, "You shall love the Lord your God with all your heart, and with all your soul, and with all your strength, and with all your mind; and your neighbor as yourself." And he said to him, "You have given the right answer; do this, and you will live."
>
> But wanting to justify himself, he asked Jesus, "And who is my neighbor?" Jesus replied, "A man was going down from Jerusalem to Jericho, and fell into the hands of robbers, who stripped him, beat him, and went away, leaving him half dead. Now by chance a priest was going down that road; and when he saw him, he passed by on the other side. So likewise a Levite, when he came to the place and saw him, passed by on the other side. But a Samaritan while traveling came near him; and when he saw him, he was moved with pity. He went to him and bandaged his wounds, having poured oil and wine on them. Then he put him on his own animal, brought him to an inn, and took care of him. The next day he took out two denarii, gave them to the innkeeper, and said, 'take care of him; and when I come back, I will repay you whatever more you spend.' Which of these three, do you think, was a neighbor to the man who fell into the hands of the robbers?" He said, "The one who showed him mercy." Jesus said to him, "Go and do likewise" (Luke 10:25–37).

Jesus chose the most foreign of outsiders to play the hero in this story, and then asked the obvious question. As I have struggled with the question, my guidance has come from the women I've gotten to know at Sagrada Familia over the last twenty years.

About thirty years ago, a new parish priest named Fr. Antonio Garcia arrived at Sagrada Familia. He had been shaped by the Catholic councils of Medellin and Puebla in the late 1960s, in which priests were encouraged to empower lay leaders in churches across Latin America. Father Garcia revolutionized the women's understanding of their own faith. He divided the parish into more than a dozen small groups, called *comunidades*. Each week, the groups of women gathered to read the Bible and to support one another. Their methodology, called the "circle of praxis" by theologians, was as simple as it was radical.

In its most basic iteration, there are three basic steps to the circle of praxis. The first is *ver* (to see). Each week, the women began by sharing stories about what had happened in their neighborhood and in their lives during the week. Who was sick? Who was out of work? Had anyone's family been touched by violence or tragedy? How were their relationships with their husbands or their kids?

The second step is *pensar* (to think). Here, the women were encouraged to read stories from the Bible and to think about the ways in which the stories they read related to their lives. What wisdom could be gleaned from the life of Jesus or from the stories of the prophets? How did Paul's letters offer insight into what the women were experiencing in their everyday lives?

The final step is *actuar* (to act). Every time they gathered, the women finished with the concrete question, "What is the text calling me to? How could we live the wisdom of the Bible in our own communities?" In the *comunidades,* the prevailing wisdom has been that you have not heard the word of God until you've taken action on it.

Today, the members of the church tell the story of those young mothers as they organized and began to gain a sense of the power of their faith witness. One of their earliest successes was to organize against an unsafe gas company that had moved into their neighborhood. The women realized their area had been targeted for the plant because no one thought they would protest. They became enraged as they investigated what actually took place at the plant and realized that it was quite dangerous and their children were at risk. Together, they inspired others from the neighborhood to join them and they marched on City Hall. Eventually the plant was moved out of their neighborhood to the outskirts of the city.

In one way or another, the women were responsible for the first schools being built in their neighborhood, for streetlights and better police protection, and for water and sewage lines being brought in.

What first drew me to Sagrada Familia was the work the women were doing with refugees. In the early 1980s Central Americans were arriving by the hundreds each week as they fled the violence of their countries and headed north for the United States. By the time they reached Agua Prieta, most were worn out, used up, broke, and exhausted. Many of the men had been beaten and robbed, and often the women had been raped. As they got off the bus in this little border city, the logical place to turn was the church.

People in Agua Prieta were as nervous about the refugees as you might expect folks would be in your own community. They didn't really understand the wars or the death squad activity in Central America, nor were they able to grasp the trauma that the refugees had been through. All they knew was that poor Central Americans were wandering around in their city, and they felt anxious about their children's safety. At Sagrada Familia, however, the women of the *comunidades* discussed the arrival of the refugees in light of stories like the Good Samaritan from Luke or the Judgment of the Nations in Matthew 25, in which Jesus makes it clear that caring for the poorest of the poor is the same as caring Christ himself.

In response, the women formed a social concerns committee to care for the refugees. Each week, a different *comunidad* took responsibility for providing food for the weary Central American travelers, who were allowed to sleep on the floor of the fellowship hall. Some of the women built relationships with doctors and nurses in town so that they could offer medical care to those who had been beaten. They held fund-raisers to buy medications. When they learned that refugees were filling the Mexican jails and had no family to provide them with food, clothing, or blankets like many of the other prisoners did, they began visiting the jail each week to offer support.

What impresses me most about the witness of these women is that every one of them was struggling to hold her own family together. These are not people who had anything extra to offer. Everything they gave was from their own limited time and even more limited household resources.

It seems to me that giving becomes easier the less one has. Two of the women in one of the *comunidades* took lessons in being good neighbors far beyond anything I have encountered anywhere else in my life. Pola and Maria (who goes by the nickname Prieta, referring to her dark skin) are *co-madres*. The literal translation of this term is "co-mother." It refers to a special relationship that neighboring women in Mexico will often grow into over time. They depend on one another for support in moments of crisis, commiserate with one another over a cup of coffee, provide childcare for one another, and tell stories. The relationship is often as close as it would be if they were sisters.

A year or two before I met Pola and Prieta, a young single mother in their neighborhood became pregnant and delivered identical twin girls, named Imelda and Esmerelda. It was obvious to Pola and Prieta that the young woman did not have the means to support the girls, so each of them volunteered to take in one of the girls and raise her as a daughter. The girls are sixteen now. They've grown up as close as sisters in houses that are a stone's throw away from one another. They have known their birth mother all of their lives, but each is quite confident of her place in Pola's and Prieta's families.

In the mid-1990s a few of the women from the church decided to begin a labor rights education project to help workers in the factories to learn exactly what their obligations and responsibilities were under Mexican labor law, and what their basic rights were as well. They began by studying the labor law themselves until several of them could literally cite it chapter and verse. Then they began knocking on doors in neighborhoods around the city. At each home, they simply asked if anyone there was working in one of the *maquiladoras*, U.S.- or foreign-owned factories. If there was, they offered a free eight- to twelve-week class to help the employees learn how to protect their rights under the law.

At first the women were discouraged because they would often offer classes for which few people would show up. Eventually they realized no one had the free time to come to a class. When they offered to come each week to meet with workers in small groups in their own homes, they discovered that there was a great deal of interest. Workers shared stories of sexual harassment, wrongful firing, forced overtime, dismissal without severance pay, unlawful pregnancy tests to determine job eligibility, and dangerous working conditions in which workers were asked to handle hazardous materials without adequate protection.

The work is quite painstaking, and it has often led to far greater demands on the women of the parish, as they've gotten involved in direct advocacy. Take the example of the firing of the workers of SewGood. This was a small, independently owned textile factory that contracted with large retail discount stores in the United States to produce products like lunch cooler bags or sports apparel. Under Mexican law, any company that fires a worker without cause is required to pay that employee a significant severance package equaling three months' wages plus a week's wage for each year the employee has been with the company. Since Mexico has no unemployment insurance, this protects the worker and enables him or her to get by until another job can be found.

In the case of SewGood and dozens of other companies like it, however, a company will often go bankrupt without holding back the money for the severance packages owed to the workers. Some ninety workers at SewGood, who arrived to find their factory abandoned one Monday morning in 1998, were collectively owed more than $250,000. At that point, their only option was to block the doors of the factory so that none of the machinery or material could be removed, with the hope that eventually they would be given permission to sell the contents of the facility for what they were owed. That process can take up to nine months or a year, and if workers take another job for a different company in the meantime, they forfeit their claim under the law.

Enter the women of the comunidades of Sagrada Familia once again. For more than eight months they collected diapers and food, sold tamales as fund-raisers, and visited the workers in their makeshift shelter in front of the factory. Once more, people who themselves live one paycheck away from disaster were the first to step up in a moment of crisis because they knew that redefinition of "neighbor" is the secret to security when one is on the economic margins of the community.

What are the lessons that can be learned from the women of Sagrada Familia?

Perhaps most important, these women have taught me that we are all connected. If there was ever a time when allegiance to a particular nation-state could supersede our allegiance to God's community, which insists that we cross borders, those days are long gone. U.S. citizens are connected in unseen ways to workers all over the world who produce what we consume. The job of church is to reach out to those who are most on the margins, wherever they may be, and to insist they be treated as brothers and sisters.

Second, service is personal. It cannot be delegated. Jesus chose the grittiest of hands-on stories to make his point about what it takes to be a neighbor to someone. We too often sanitize our picture of the man left beaten beside the road. One might reasonably expect that he was filthy. He had no money. Who knows what he did to provoke the beating he received? Most of us who have grown up with privilege and comfort today would have crossed to the other side of the street in order not to have contact with the man. Yet the women of Sagrada Familia know that the *first* act of faithfulness in our world today is to place ourselves in situations where we *will* come to know people on the margins and in communities where we might not normally feel comfortable. Over and over, they make it clear that our task is to see Jesus in the face of each person we meet. They have taught me that it is impossible to be a neighbor to someone without a personal relationship with that person.

Third, caring for others is a community project. We must place ourselves in communities that will nurture in us a commitment to support others who are in need and enable us to act on that commitment. Perhaps we need to adopt the notion of *co-madres* or *co-padres* and find ways to deepen our friendships beyond casual social interactions to the more profound challenges of engaging the world. The experience of living in poverty makes obvious what too many of us have long since forgotten in the United States. None of us, no matter who we are or where we live, are capable of this kind of faithful discipleship as individuals. This kind of work demands that we depend upon one another and support one another. As obvious as that is in a community like Agua Prieta, it seems to be the hardest thing to imagine for those of us who live in communities of wealth.

But let us not kid ourselves. There is a reason why this intimate expression of "neighbor" tends to happen in communities like the barrios of Agua Prieta. As we begin to develop a sense of economic independence from one another, we tend to isolate ourselves from real interaction. Often, getting close at this level involves sharing and taking responsibility for one another's pain and struggle. Sometimes I have watched as the women of the *comunidades* get frustrated with one another. We are all human, and relationship is likely to involve difficulty. On the other hand, the payoff for practicing this kind of community is significant. I have been blessed to watch as the relationships between these women have matured and deepened over many years.

On the global level, everything about who we are in the United States today is working against this radical notion of "neighbor." If we choose to practice the kind of radical hospitality that Jesus insisted upon in the story of the Good Samaritan, we will at best be called idealistic and naïve; it is even possible we will be told that we are traitors, supporters of terrorism, and unpatriotic. It is clear, however, that there has never been a more important time to redefine "neighbor" using gospel values.

In the end, answering the question "Who is my neighbor?" hinges on allegiance. To whom do I owe care and concern? Whom will I invite into my community? How far will I go in my notion of a church that follows Jesus Christ into the world to seek out neighbors like the man beaten and left for dead beside the road?

The women of Sagrada Familia are older now. Many of them are helping to raise grandchildren while their sons and daughters work in the factories. There is a noticeable lack of participation of the younger generation in the weekly meetings of the *comunidades*, although the church is in many ways more vibrant than ever. Few people have the time for a weekly Bible study nowadays, but there is an active crew of volunteers who continue to provide for the basic needs of migrants who arrive each day looking for a place to stay. The church now operates a dormitory and a dining hall as well as a small human rights office. The hands-on work of providing hospitality has attracted younger couples and even some teenagers, and the church is finding new life based on the same gospel principles as always:

Recognize the overwhelming need in the world around you.
Study the Bible.
Take action to live what you believe.

This seems to me like the right prescription for renewing the church and transforming the politics of our time.

Women, Childbearing, and Justice

CHLOE BREYER

Male and female created he them.

—*Genesis 1:27*

During a summer of chaplaincy training at Bellevue Hospital in New York City, my fellow chaplain-in-training encountered a young woman and her mother in the recovery ward of the hospital. The young woman had just had an abortion. Recounting the encounter in the context of group supervision, my colleague surmised that the girl's socially ambitious mother had pressured her daughter into having an abortion to escape the social stigma of unwed motherhood. In the course of their conversation, the young woman disclosed to my colleague that she had been pregnant with twins. This knowledge compounded and accentuated the young woman's sadness and confusion at that moment. My colleague, who shares my belief in a woman's legal right to choose an abortion, wondered what would have happened if this particular young woman had had a chance for guided moral reflection before her fateful decision rather than afterward.

This young woman, the subject of a clinical pastoral training discussion, is also the symbolic focus of a public clash of values. She and others in her position have been picketed, legislated for, preached at, and alternately championed or vilified in public forums around our country for more than forty years. Almost always, she and her decision are lamented and even scorned by the members of the "pro-life" religious Right, a group whose views have come to be seen as synonymous with "moral" in the public eye. Rarely, if ever, do spokespersons for this perspective appear to view the young woman as endowed with full moral agency or as making a decision within a unique circumstance that may also be colored by extenuating circumstances. Hardly ever do these pro-life advocates place a woman's decision about whether to abort a fetus in the category where it properly belongs: in the category of all challenging, quintessentially human moral decisions.

But is a woman capable of moral discernment? Absurd as it may seem, a significant part of the worldwide Christian church still believes a woman is *not* capable, or at the very least is *less* capable. In this they miss the extraordinary example of Jesus, who actually heeds what a woman has to say—who is in fact even *shamed* by what a woman has to say.

I am referring to the remarkable account given in Matthew 15—also told in more compressed form in Mark 7—of the so-called Syro-Phoenician woman (Matthew and Mark disagree on whether she should be called a Canaanite or a Greek, but their point is identical: she isn't Jewish) who approaches Jesus when he happens to appear within her home region.

Matthew's account is the more dramatic, with more dialogue filled in, but Mark's is more interesting on account of the revealing detail that Jesus was trying to *hide* in this extreme northern region of Palestine: "And he entered a house and would not have any one know it: yet he could not be hid. But immediately a woman whose little daughter was possessed..." (24–25).

What makes this detail in Mark especially revealing is that the story of this encounter with the woman follows a passage in which Jesus proclaims: "What comes out of a man is what defiles a man. For from within, out of the heart of man, come evil thoughts, fornication, theft, murder, adultery, coveting, wickedness, deceit, licentiousness, envy, slander, pride, foolishness. All of these evil things come from within, and they defile a man." Jesus said all this to rebuke the Pharisees, who had complained that the disciples ate with unwashed (i.e., defiled) hands. So Jesus, having made the speech and then having tried to hide, has set himself up for a test of exactly what goodness or what "evil things" lie within his own heart.

And he does not, at first, pass the test! The woman cries out for mercy, falling at his feet and telling the story of her tormented daughter.

"But he did not answer her a word," according to Matthew, while meanwhile his disciples are urging him to send this whining intruder away.

Matthew is specific on the reason for Jesus's stony response; Matthew has Jesus say, "I was sent only to the lost sheep of Israel." Therefore, he continues, it is "not *fair* to take the children's bread and throw it to the dogs." This morally vacant statement provokes the woman to answer from the depths of her heart: "Yes, Lord, yet even the dogs eat the crumbs that fall from their master's table." Mark's rendering is still sharper: "Yes, Lord, yet even the dogs under the table eat the children's crumbs."

In the end, Jesus cannot resist this woman's moral reasoning. Mark has him replying, "For this saying you may go your way; the demon has left your daughter." Matthew's version here is perhaps more to the point: "O woman, great is your faith! Be it done for you as you desire."

In this essay I am seeking to establish beyond any doubt a woman's capacity for moral discernment. It is well past time that the recognition experienced by Jesus is experienced with equal force by his whole church.

Building on the work of a growing number of theologians and clerics who question the idea that a pro-life position is the only moral position for people of faith, I wish to present a constructive alternative way for religious leaders to engage women who are confronting the question of what to do in the face of an unwanted pregnancy. As an Episcopal priest and also a mother of two, I will draw on my personal and pastoral experience to suggest a set of questions for reflection that women of faith and their pastors might explore together when facing the decision of whether to abort a fetus. At the same time, I hope to challenge some "pro-choice" supporters who have, unwittingly or not, allowed the language of choice to be too closely associated with the idea of mere personal preference and with the non-ethics of a materialistic and self-serving popular culture. In all of this I will seek to recall and apply the spirit of the Jesus who, at his best, never condemns any woman but who holds all individuals to account for the moral meaning of their lives.

While the parallels between a woman's decision between competing goods in a private context (the good of the unborn child's life vs. the good of the mother's—and in many cases the whole family's—quality of existence) and a government official's decision regarding war in the public realm are not perfect, they are worth contemplating in light of the church's historic refusal to see women as endowed with the same moral decision-making capabilities as men. The issues I will be exploring are not intended to create a litmus test for legal decisions governing abortion; rather, I hope this discussion may offer some guidance to women of faith and their spiritual guides in wrestling with one of life's most difficult decisions: a decision that, to take the assumptions of the most ardent pro-lifers, does indeed affect the community at large and that also, like the decision to wage a war, brings with it social as well as personal consequences. Ultimately, remembering an unhappy woman in the recovery ward of Bellevue Hospital, I hope to reclaim a woman's right to choose as a deeply reflective process that can be rooted in her faith and contribute to her spiritual growth. Such a process ought to draw upon all of the scriptural resources, theological tools, and pastoral understanding that communities of faith have to offer.

Needed: Sound Justice Criteria for Abortion Decisions

Churches, and the Roman Catholic Church in particular, have long offered members guidance in making moral decisions when it comes to actions in public life. Just-war doctrine is one such body of teaching that has helped statesmen determine when it is legitimate to wage war—an action that always risks not only the lives of soldiers but that increasingly puts civilian lives at risk as well. While just-war theory has evolved over the centuries from a duty-based to a rights-based doctrine, the justice criteria still require the decision-making actor to address several important questions. Historically, that actor is a male in a position of public trust, and the key questions he must answer are these: Does he have the authority to declare war? What are the primary *causes* for using force on such a large scale? Do those causes outweigh the suffering that a war will wreak on soldiers and civilians? Have all other avenues of conflict resolution been exhausted before organized violence is employed?

A public official's consideration of each of these questions was deemed highly important over the last seventeen centuries, and not only for ensuring cooperation from the parliament and exchequer or for securing the full blessing of the church hierarchy. Faithful consideration of these key questions was also thought to matter for the good of the ruler's soul.

From the perspective of a woman of faith who has an unwanted pregnancy and who faces the decision of whether to have an abortion, several of these same questions may help to guide her in determining a course of action. While the decision to have an abortion is always difficult to describe as "good," in many situations that decision can certainly be described as just. Carefully processing the questions of justice in relation to herself, to other family members, and to the future of the child she might bear may provide a woman with helpful direction.

Legitimate Authority

Who has the authority to decide whether to end an unwanted pregnancy? From a perspective of faith, is the pregnant woman herself the final decision maker rather than an external religious or legal authority? No one has the authority to take another's life, even if that "life" is unborn, says one conservative set of public religious perspectives. To talk about a woman's *authority* in this matter of abortion the same as legitimizing murder. According to this point of view, only a moral relativist or materialist with no respect for the sanctity of human life would do such a thing.

Without entering the debate about when life begins, I believe these voices of the religious Right should be heard with skepticism in light of the checkered historical record that the church, its teachings, and its representatives have had in recognizing the full humanity of women. The centuries-old double standard that is evinced when religious leaders extend their blessing to public officials leading their troops off to war, while offering only harsh condemnation to women seeking abortion, invites healthy suspicion of all Christian Right arguments against abortion, not to say the shrill moralism that accompanies these arguments.

I have already made it clear that the analogy between a political leader entrusted with life-and-death decisions and a pregnant woman entrusted with the fate of an unborn child is imperfect. Nonetheless, the analogy is worth exploring in light of the church's long history of denying women's moral agency.

Aristotle's notion that "the deliberative part of woman's soul [is] impotent" and in need of supervision has shaped women's status throughout Western history inside and outside the churches. As recently as a century ago, serious academic discussion mulled the danger of education to women's reproductive functioning. Far from rejecting these misconceptions, early founders of the Christian Church helped to fuel them. Many of the early church fathers, influenced by Greek culture, absorbed the notion of dualism between mind and body and created a hierarchical patterning of "the spiritual male mind" over against the "carnal female body."

St. Augustine, drawing on a metaphor found in Ephesians 5:23, interpreted St. Paul to mean that the woman had no head of her own, but that her husband was to be her head, as she was to be his body. Ten centuries later, Martin Luther found women deficient in their capacity to image God because of the role of Eve in the Fall. Thus Luther in "Lectures on Genesis": "Although a most extraordinary creature similar to Adam, as far as the image of God is concerned, she was nevertheless a woman." In Luther's view, any woman's unwillingness to accept the subordinate role in relationship to men was a rebellion against her place as a domestic creature in relation to man.

While this unequal view of men and women has changed for the better over time—witness the introduction of inclusive language, the changing role of women's leadership, and the ordination of women within most Protestant denominations—echoes of this view still reverberate in church life. They affect everything from pastoral approaches to domestic violence to the debate over women's ordination in the Roman Catholic and Orthodox traditions. It goes without saying that this inheritance strongly affects Roman Catholic and conservative evangelical teachings on abortion.

In an important essay on the theology and morality of procreative choice that is included in a volume titled *Making the Connections*, Beverly Wildung Harrison and Shirley Cloys note that the Roman Catholic Church's current teachings on abortion selectively apply the doctrine of *imagio dei* (the principle that all human beings are made in the image of God). Harrison and Cloys argue that in the case of Roman Catholic teachings, treating abortion an as abstract act divorced from the particular concerns of the woman who is pregnant, while at the same time affording men in public trust "vast moral range in relation to justifiable homicide" (i.e., war making), discloses the continuation of an ancient belief that women are less equipped or less qualified than men to make difficult and potentially life-threatening moral decisions.

The church's silence on the nature of the mitigating complex circumstances that might lead a woman to choose abortion, and its abstract historic focus on the personhood of a fetus, contrast sharply with the same Catholic Church's nuanced treatment of complex circumstances facing public officials as they weigh the use of force. This deep inconsistency denies the capability of an adult woman to make moral decisions, just as it gives wide-ranging powers of moral decision making to males. The dissonance calls into question the church's professed belief that men and women are fully and equally created in God's image. It applies a biological reductionism to one gender that is not applied to the other.

"The distinctly human power," write Harrison and Cloys, "is not our biologic capacity to bear children, but our power to actively love, nurture, care for one another and shape one another's existence in cultural and social interactions. To equate a biologic process with full normative humanity is crass biologic reductionism, and such reductionism is never practiced in religious ethics except where women's lives and well-being are involved."

Margaret Sanger, the founder of Planned Parenthood, found that her most serious arguments with the Roman Catholic Church were not so much about freeing women from motherhood (as her modern-day detractors within the religious Right have alleged) but were about church teachings that destroy women's authority—not only in public life and leadership but even in the area of their own reproductive lives. Christianity's greatest outrage against women was forbidding them to control the function of motherhood under any circumstances: this demeaned women's humanity.

"In the moral code developed by the Church," Sanger wrote in her 1922 *Pivot of Civilization*, "women have been so degraded that they have been habituated to look upon themselves through the eyes of men... we are not passive machines.... We are alive and intelligent... and we must awaken to the essential realization that we are living beings, endowed with will, choice, comprehension."

In a society in which the parents have primary responsibility for a child's upbringing, legitimate authority over whether a child is to be carried to full term *must* rest with the mother. Both pro-life and pro-choice advocates agree that a forced abortion, either state-coerced or urged by another outside authority, is illegitimate. And in this regard, inadequate recognition of the historical association of abortion with forced sterilization along with the phenomenon of abortion for the sake of gender selection can make pro-choice arguments appear parochial at times. While Margaret Sanger was clear on this point, she also took issue with proponents of the eugenics movement who believed some women should bear as many children as possible as a duty to the state: "A woman possessing an adequate knowledge of her reproductive functions is the best judge of the time and conditions under which her child should be brought into the world... and [furthermore] it is her right to determine whether she shall bear children or not."

But if a woman is the ultimate authority in the decision on whether to end an unwanted pregnancy, what about society's collective responsibility for maternal care? Concerns about this and other pro-choice arguments are highlighted by Roman Catholic scholars and activists in a book entitled *The Cost of Choice*. The "pro-abortionist" position, according to contributor Elizabeth Fox-Genovese, uncritically accepts a worldview that is dedicated to "instant gratification and disdain for sacrifice, and perhaps most portentously, its abandonment of children." This "embrace of women's right to the anxious freedom of disconnected individualism," continues Fox-Genovese, "has effectively deprived women of the protection and support that pregnancy and maternity require."

But upholding women as fully capable moral agents should not in any way threaten a social safety net created to protect society's most vulnerable. The elderly, for example, do not have their rights taken away when they become more dependent on hospital or hospice care and thus require more of society's collective resources for support than they did as younger people. Likewise, any argument that women must choose between having full authority when it comes to deciding the fate of a fetus and having access to good maternal health care is disingenuous. While improved maternal health care and services for poor mothers may indeed reduce the number of abortions, this does not mean that an *increase* in the abortion rate can or should bring about a reduction in the resources society allocates for maternal care.

Just Cause

In *The City of God*, St. Augustine describes two cities—one of heaven and one of earth. As denizens of the heavenly city, Christians are to spend their lives as strangers or pilgrims in the earthly city, recognizing its imperfect and unjust quality while remembering that this place is not their true home. This worldview allows a Christian to be a judge who, fulfilling his earthly responsibilities, may condemn criminals to death. This worldview also recognizes that public officials may at times employ force to protect the citizens whom they are entrusted to govern, even if employing such force leads to the suffering of certain innocents.

While the *City of God* obviously does not address the situation of a woman who faces an unwanted pregnancy, Augustine's public theology nevertheless has bearing on the kind of choice a woman of faith who has become pregnant—unwillingly, unknowingly, or in ignorance of planning—may make in deciding whether to have an abortion.

What are the circumstances in which a woman of faith might decide to have an abortion? We are familiar with the ethical dilemma faced by a male policy maker whose decisions affect the lives of innocent people. But what of the pregnant woman pondering the future of the child she is carrying and the fate of her family were she to bring that child to term? What if the birth of an additional child will mean aggravating the effects of poverty for its brother or sister? Suppose the caretaking needs of an additional younger sibling will mean limiting educational opportunities for an older one?

In her work on this subject, Beverley Harrison carefully describes the situations in which she believes a woman's decision to have an abortion must be considered just. Here I expand on her core insights.

Sexual violence. When pregnancy is the result of sexual violence of any kind, an abortion, if chosen by the woman, is always just. Harrison goes so far as to say that *not* allowing the mother to choose abortion is a cruel continuation of the crime, whether committed by a husband, a stranger, or a family member. It is the ultimate instance of blaming the victim.

The mother's health. One of the only passages in the Bible that speaks directly to the question of the value of life before birth is found in Exodus 21:22: "When people who are fighting injure a pregnant woman so that there is a miscarriage, and yet no further harm follows, the one responsible shall be fined what the woman's husband demands, paying as much as the judges determine." If the woman had died, however, the injury done to her would call for capital punishment under the principle of a life for a life. The degrees of punishment in these two cases show that the life of the woman was always of greater value than that of the unborn child—a child who, even in the last trimester, has lesser moral status than the woman, who has developed relationships in the world. When the mother's health is endangered, a fetus may even be dismembered in order to save her life. According to the influential teacher Rashi, a fetus is not fully human (i.e., not yet a *nefesh*) until the head has emerged in the birthing process.

Ignorance. According to a traditional understanding of natural law, moral culpability requires foreknowledge. Thus, a young girl who participates in heterosexual activity without clear knowledge of how pregnancy occurs or without intending to conceive a child would, by traditional natural law standards, be held to be in a state of ignorance and not "culpable" morally. Harrison gives an account of one Roman Catholic nun who believes that her church "should not consider the abortions of young Catholic girls as morally culpable because the Church had overprotected them, denied them knowledge of their reproductive function, which contributed to their lack of understanding of procreation and to their inability to cope with the sexual pressures girls experience in contemporary society."

Extreme poverty. Here again Margaret Sanger's story is still relevant. Sanger described the conditions she encountered as a nurse in some of the ten thousand apartments on the Lower East Side of Manhattan that housed a deadly mixture of poverty, ignorance, and overcrowding: "women writhing in travail to bring forth little babies; the babies themselves naked and hungry, wrapped in newspapers to keep them from the cold; six-year-old children with pinched faces . . . old in concentrated wretchedness, pushed into grey and fetid cellars . . . their small scrawny hands scuttling through rags making lampshades, artificial flowers, [and] coffins."

Sanger began her work in birth control in response to this overwhelming poverty, this hopelessness, and the deadly forms of abortion women then sought in order to relieve their families of distress. Sanger did not act out of a desire for self-enrichment or self-aggrandizement, as today's antiabortion advocates often insinuate. In her autobiography, Sanger evokes the moment that converted her to what would become a lifelong campaign for reproductive rights and education.

One evening in 1912 Sanger received a call from a tenement on Grand Street. When she arrived, she found a young Russian woman and mother of three dying from a self-induced abortion. For three weeks, she and a doctor battled the infection; finally, the woman recovered. Sanger's autobiography recalls the plea the woman made for information that would help her prevent another pregnancy. "You want your cake and eat it too? That's impossible," the doctor replied flippantly: "Go and tell Jake to sleep on the roof." The woman waited until the doctor left before turning to Sanger to plead for "the secret." Sanger promised to return but procrastinated, knowing that there was no information she could provide that would give the woman what she wanted. When Sanger did return three months later, she was responding to another desperate call from the woman's frantic husband. This time, the mother died within ten minutes of Sanger's arrival. Sanger wrote that she went to bed that night "knowing that no matter what it might cost, I was finished with palliatives and superficial cures; I was resolved to seek out the root of evil, to do something to change the destiny of mothers whose miseries were as vast as the skies."

When a woman struggles to feed, clothe, and provide the material basics for herself and the children that she already has, and when the birth of another child would clearly endanger the lives of other members of her family, safe abortion must be considered a just option.

Disability of the fetus. This is now contested terrain. In an essay in *The Cost of Choice* about her decision to carry a child with Down syndrome to full term, law professor Elizabeth Schlitz argues that widespread acceptance of genetic abortion has "caused far too many to view human life through the lens of a cost-benefit analysis," which expects a mother to abort a child she knows is disabled. While it is true that too much of modern life is viewed through such a lens, it is still unclear why Schlitz should raise genetic abortion as the most blatant example of the expedient way human life is treated in our time, rather than focusing, say, on deadly sweatshop conditions for workers overseas or the growing use of capital punishment in the United States.

Harrison describes two other situations in which a woman could, in her view, decide to have an abortion. These are *contraceptive failure* and *social pressure* on women not to use contraception. Though plausible, these situations seem less clear-cut than others. While it is not fair to penalize the woman who was seeking to prevent an unintended/unwanted pregnancy and experienced contraceptive failure through no fault of her own, suppose this failure occurs in the context of a happy marriage? Unintended or not, if another child would not endanger the well-being of the family, abortion might not be the right answer. Likewise, a woman who is aware of the risks of not using birth control but who nevertheless bends to social pressure not to use it, might rightly be seen to be evading personal responsibility.

Last Resort

The last-resort question asks: Have all other possible avenues for achieving moral goals been exhausted? Is there someone else in the mother's life with time, resources, and willingness to care for the child should she choose to keep it? Might carrying the child to full term and putting it up for adoption be an option, given the circumstances? Is the mother in a marriage or relationship that can sustain her and provide the care necessary for her child? How will this decision affect a mother's ability to reflect the image of God in her own life and actions? Obviously these are questions most women can and should ponder carefully before deciding to abort a fetus, and the Christian community should help provide opportunities for such reflection.

Reasonable Hope of Success and Proportionality

In just-war theory, both of these requirements can be summarized in the following questions: Will the value of your action outweigh the intermediate costs? Will the ends justify the means? In just-war theory, if resorting to armed violence will only increase the number of casualties and create a further distance from the just peace that is its purported purpose, then resorting to war is not acceptable. This is the counsel of prudence.

In the case of a woman deciding what to do about an unwanted pregnancy, prudence requires that she know herself and her own temperament. Many studies and reports have shown situations where a woman deeply regrets having an abortion long after the event, even if she believed it to be the correct course of action at the time. Even if the circumstances in a woman's life are such that an abortion would be a just option, do her own personality, belief system, instincts, and character suggest that she will be able to live well with her decision? Again, one longs for a society in which religiously grounded resources—supportive resources, not condemnation—would be available to help women work through the prudential question.

Toward Equality and Responsibility

Unlike the just-war criteria, these reflections about just abortion do not offer a strict test but do offer a set of questions or guidelines that a pregnant woman as moral decision maker can consult as she seeks to determine a path of action. They offer an alternative to the habit of choosing according to pleasure or whim, as one does in the cereal aisle, which is how the pro-life forces caricature those who ultimately choose abortion. The justice criteria recognize the worth of prayerful contemplation in the context of rational guidelines. This, if nothing else, will help the decision maker to pause before acting and thus reduce the likelihood that an important and life-determining step will be taken in haste or out of fear alone. Finally, a justice criterion for abortion will also offer a woman faced with the choice of aborting or keeping a child the sense that she is not alone. It will help show her that she is making a decision that is qualitatively similar to others that men and women of faith have had to make over the course of history. Like just-war theory, this set of guidelines recognizes that it is impossible for people of faith—men and women—to "wash their hands" morally in certain cases. Being made in the image of God entails acting and deciding under imperfect circumstances and taking full responsibility for one's actions nonetheless.

However imperfect, the criteria derived from just-war teaching do offer guidance and support in an arena where these have been sorely lacking. While many would say it is hard to find very much justice at all in practices of modern warfare, the rich ethical resources historically developed by the church in relation to ethical warrants for war making retain significant value in this other arena. For far too long, and contrary to Jesus's example, the church denied the full humanity of women gifted with the biological capacity to bear children. The church gave unwarranted preference to male humanity over female humanity. In so doing, the church dishonored the core biblical teaching that all human beings are made in the image of God. It is time to mitigate that wrong and to support and empower the full moral discernment of women.

Burying the Executioner's Ax: A Christian Rejection of Capital Punishment

PATRICK McCORMICK

But I say to you, do not retaliate by evil means.

—*Matthew* 5:39

Not Your Ancestors' Death Penalty

In the past half century most of the major Christian bodies in America have come out against the death penalty. But church leaders and theologians calling for the abolition of capital punishment have had to face three challenges. First, even as a rising tide of churches took public stands against the death penalty, an increasing majority of American Christians reported that they support capital punishment. By the late 1990s roughly three-quarters of Americans claimed to support the death penalty. Second, most of these Christians (and most major Christian thinkers who have written on this topic in the last two millennia) see their position as grounded in the Bible. And third, the churches' current opposition to capital punishment reverses long-standing ecclesiastical support that reaches back at least to Ambrose and Augustine in the fourth century. As a result, Christian opponents of the death penalty find themselves faced with a widely popular practice that appears to be firmly grounded in both scripture and tradition.

By itself, the current widespread support for the death penalty among American Christians is not an insuperable obstacle. There was a time when most American Christians supported slavery and opposed giving women the vote. And as recently as the 1970s most Americans *opposed* the death penalty. Hearts and minds can be changed, particularly if people are presented with persuasive arguments and information regarding the harms and injustices of capital punishment, and particularly if they are offered realistic alternatives that ensure fit punishment for serious crimes and adequate protections for the community.

A recent survey of American Catholics indicates that a twenty-five-year campaign by the U.S. Conference of Catholic Bishops (with a good deal of help from people like Sr. Helen Prejean) has helped cut Catholic support for the death penalty from a recent high of 68 percent to just 48 percent. Pollster John Zogby reports that a third of U.S. Catholics who once supported the death penalty now oppose it and that support for the death penalty drops among Catholics as church attendance increases. Clearly, congregations can be persuaded by good theological and moral arguments.

The fact that Christians have long used the Bible to justify the death penalty does not prove capital punishment is moral or Christian. Biblical passages have been cited in defense of slavery, segregation, and unspeakably violent crusades. Still, the long-standing use of the Bible to justify capital punishment does require that Christian abolitionists address scriptural texts and present persuasive biblical arguments against capital punishment.

But death penalty proponents must also acknowledge a serious problem with using the Bible to defend capital punishment, which is that hardly any of them would support what the Bible actually has to say about putting people to death. No serious Christians would consent to executing people for committing the more than two dozen offenses listed as capital crimes in the Bible—offenses including sorcery, improper touching of tabernacle furniture, blasphemy, profaning the Sabbath, false prophesy, idolatry, bearing false witness, kidnapping, negligent homicide, rebelling against one's parents, contempt of court, keeping dangerous livestock, adultery, bestiality, male homosexual relations, prostitution, sexual relations during menstruation, incest, rape, and falsely claiming to be a virgin at the time of one's marriage.

And no serious Christian proponents of capital punishment would permit death row inmates to be stoned, burned, decapitated, strangled, or crucified. Indeed, hardly any would support public executions in the town square or at the city gate, as biblically prescribed.

Curiously enough, modern Christian proponents of the death penalty also tend to reject biblical requirements that no one be put to death without the testimony of two eyewitnesses (Deuteronomy 19:15 and Numbers 35:30), or that the rich not be able to "ransom" their way out of an execution (Numbers 35:31). Those who cite "an eye for an eye" rarely complain about people being executed based on circumstantial evidence or about the overwhelming number of the poor on death row.

Nor does the long tradition of Christian support for capital punishment prove that the practice is right, particularly if—as many of these churches now believe—the circumstances have changed. Christians no longer believe that slavery or segregation is right, or that charging interest on a loan (i.e., usury) is wrong. Still, reversing a tradition reaching back nearly two millennia requires a set of persuasive arguments.

And again, Christian proponents who turn to medieval and ancient authorities to justify the death penalty would almost certainly reject the extensive use and barbaric forms of this penalty that were readily accepted by our religious forebears. Hardly any contemporary Christians would support executing people for the nearly 350 capital crimes found in Britain at the time of the American Revolution—offenses including petty theft, counterfeiting stamps, killing rabbits, or cutting down trees in a public park. Nor would they tolerate people being boiled in oil, flayed alive, burned at the stake, impaled, drawn and quartered, beheaded, or tortured on the rack. Most would find it abhorrent to execute children as young as eight or mentally retarded persons incapable of understanding the crimes they are accused of committing.

Thus, while Christian proponents might argue that the Bible and tradition are on their side, hardly any modern Christian proponents of the death penalty would defend the broad and savage uses of this punishment as described in the Bible or as sanctioned by Christians of earlier ages. The conflict is not between those who wish to be faithful to the

Bible and Christian tradition and those who would flout these sources. Rather, the debate is about whether the evolving Christian stance on the death penalty should now, at long last, embrace abolition.

The Shifting Tide of History

History seems to be clearly on the side of the abolitionists. Most nations and churches have turned against what was long a universal practice; in places where it still takes place the list of capital crimes has now shrunk to a handful of offenses, and nearly all the traditional forms of execution have been eliminated.

When Cesare Beccaria wrote the first modern assault on the death penalty in 1764, no nation condemned the practice. But by 1871 five European nations had either abolished or discontinued the practice. By the 1960s France, Ireland, Spain, and Greece were the only non-Communist European nations that had not abolished the death penalty, and even these countries had practically eliminated its use. By 2004 there were 84 nations that had abolished the death penalty for all crimes, and the tally of those that had eliminated capital punishment in practice was up to 120. Only 76 countries still retain and use the death penalty, and in each of the last five years fewer than half of them have actually put someone to death. Indeed, for several years over 90 percent of executions have taken place in just four nations: China, Iran, Vietnam, and the United States.

Four international treaties now call for the abolition of capital punishment. The Second Optional Protocol to the United Nations' International Covenant on Civil and Political Rights and the Protocol to the American Convention on Human Rights to Abolish the Death Penalty call for the complete elimination of the death penalty, with a possible exception for wartime crimes. Protocol No. 6 to the European Convention for the Protection of Human Rights and Fundamental Freedoms calls for the abolition of the death penalty in peacetime, and Protocol

No. 13 to the European Convention for the Protection of Human Rights and Fundamental Freedoms calls for the complete abolition of capital punishment.

Although most Christian churches had long accepted capital punishment, nearly all the mainline denominations in the United States have now called for an end to the death penalty. This cloud of witnesses includes the American Baptists, the General Conference of General Baptists, the Church of the Brethren, the Bruderhof Communities, the Disciples of Christ, the Episcopal Church USA, the Evangelical Lutheran Church, the General Conference Mennonite Church, the Orthodox Church in America, the United Methodist Church, the Moravian Church, the Presbyterian Church (USA), the Reformed Church in America, the U.S. Conference of Catholic Bishops, the Society of Friends (Quakers), the Unitarian Universalist Church, the United Church of Christ, and the National Council of the Churches of Christ.

Even in the United States, the world's fourth leading practitioner of capital punishment, support is weakening. More than 1,000 persons have been executed since the death penalty was reintroduced in 1976, and over 3,400 prisoners currently await execution. Still, the number of persons executed in 2004 was the lowest since 1998, and the number sentenced to death was the lowest since 1976. Until recently the United States led the world in the execution of juvenile offenders, but in 2005 the Supreme Court ruled that putting such persons to death was unconstitutional, and in 2002 the high court finally outlawed the execution of the mentally retarded. Throughout the nation juries in every state but Texas and New Mexico are now offered—and increasingly choose—the option of imposing a life sentence without parole.

Biblical Arguments

Christian support for capital punishment has long relied on a handful of biblical passages: Genesis 9:6, Exodus 21:23–25, and Romans 13:1–7. Before addressing those passages and offering some biblical arguments against capital punishment, we should note several points.

First, all of the biblical passages calling for the death penalty "are found in the first five books of the Bible; none appears in the prophets, the writings, or the New Testament, which do not teach the death penalty."[1] Indeed, not only does the New Testament fail to "teach the death penalty," but Jesus's radical and consistent demand that his followers reject vengeance and embrace forgiveness places a major roadblock in the way of any Christian attempt to construct a biblical justification for capital punishment.

Second, much of the Mosaic Law regarding the death penalty was meant to reduce the level of violence in society, preventing escalating blood feuds that avenged their victims seven- or seventyfold. These passages were not written to command that a life be taken for a life, but to forbid anyone from ever taking *more than one* life.

Third, it is not clear ancient Israelites understood these biblical passages as requiring them to actually execute offenders. Leading rabbinic scholars of the second century of the common era argued that biblical mandates about capital punishment were a symbolic reminder of the importance of following God's law, but that other legal and moral requirements made it practically impossible to execute anyone.[2]

Fourth, for three centuries after the death of Jesus, leading Christian authors argued that Christians were forbidden to participate in the death penalty. Even though writers like Justin Martyr, Tertullian, Origen, and Cyprian of Carthage accepted the state's authority to execute criminals, they argued that Christians could not in conscience order or carry out such killings.[3]

PASSAGES IN SUPPORT OF CAPITAL PUNISHMENT

Genesis 9:6

"If anyone sheds the blood of man, by man shall his blood be shed; for in the image of God has man been made." For centuries Christian proponents of the death penalty have argued that this passage relates God's command to execute murderers. But contemporary biblical scholarship has shown that Genesis 9:6 is not a piece of divine legislation at all but a proverb. Unlike biblical legislation, the passage is written in poetic form and does not express God's command to execute murderers; rather, it reflects human wisdom about what happens to those who turn to violence—"they reap what they sow."

Jesus utters a nearly identical proverb in Matthew 26:52, instructing his disciple to put away his sword, "for all who take the sword will perish by the sword." In what biblical scholars claim is Jesus's own interpretation of Genesis 9:6, Christ warns his disciple against the use of violence because it only begets more bloodshed—not because God commands that he be executed.

Of course, if Genesis 9:6 is a divine command, it demands more than the execution of murderers. If "anyone" who takes a human life must be put to death, there is to be no exception for those who accidentally take a life or for children or for the mentally incompetent.

Moreover, Genesis 9:6 does not call upon the government to carry out these executions but rather presumes that the victim's relatives will avenge themselves. This means that Genesis 9:6 would not authorize the death penalty but *would* authorize blood feuds and gang wars.

Exodus 21:23–25

Christian proponents of capital punishment have long argued that putting murderers to death is justified by the Bible's call for "life for life, eye for eye, [and] tooth for tooth," which is found in Exodus 21:23–25, Leviticus 24:19, and Deuteronomy 19:19–21. According to the *lex talionis*, or law of retaliation, retributive and biblical justice demand a punishment that matches the crime; capital punishment is thus viewed as the penalty that best responds to murder. Take a life, lose a life, the argument goes.

The first problem with the "eye for an eye" defense is that the lex talionis was not meant to defend capital punishment against those calling for mercy or forgiveness but rather to restrain those calling for vengeance. The biblical command about a life for a life and an eye for an eye forbids victims and their families from taking seven or seventy lives for a life; it was meant to interrupt the escalating violence of blood feuds, not to command that all killers be executed.

A second problem is that even the passages calling for retaliation do not apply a rule of exact retribution. Immediately following Exodus 21:23–25, we read that slaves losing an eye or tooth from a beating should be set free, not that the master should lose his eye or tooth. Just before Leviticus 24:19 the Lord commands that those who curse God are to be stoned, not cursed in return. And in Deuteronomy 19:19–21 the punishment for false testimony is not to have lies told about you but to be put to death. The law of retaliation calls for punishments that fit (and do not exceed) the crime but not necessarily for penalties that exactly mirror the original offense.

The third problem with the "eye for an eye" argument is no one today believes we should actually take out the eye of someone who has blinded another person, or punish anyone by taking a "tooth for tooth, hand for hand, [or] foot for foot." Nor do we any longer believe in imposing a "burn for burn, bruise for bruise, wound for wound." We do not beat assailants, rape rapists, molest molesters, burn arsonists, or torture torturers (or at least we ought not to do so). We do not impose these kinds of penalties because we find them brutal and barbaric; because we do not wish to become rapists, torturers, molesters, arsonists, or assailants ourselves; and because we do not wish to ask other people to become rapists or torturers on our behalf.

Still, the most serious problem with any Christian using "an eye for and eye" to defend capital punishment is that Jesus completely reformed this rule. In Matthew 5:38–39 Jesus tells his audience, "You have heard that it was said, 'an eye for an eye, and a tooth for a tooth.' But I say to you, do not retaliate by evil means." Instead of a burn for a burn and a stripe for a stripe, Christians are to turn the other cheek, to hand over their cloak, and to walk the extra mile. They are to resist evil not by mirroring the violence of their enemies but by interrupting the cycle of violence through transformative acts that oppose evil and injustice without succumbing to vengeful and violent means.

Romans 13:3–4

"For rulers hold no terror for those who do right, but for those who do wrong. Do you want to be free from fear of the one in authority? Then do what is right and he will commend you. For he is God's servant to do you good. But if you do wrong, be afraid, for he does not bear the sword for nothing. He is God's servant, an agent of wrath to bring punishment on the wrongdoer."

Christian defenses of capital punishment have relied upon Romans 13 more than any other New Testament passage, arguing that Paul recognizes the state's right to punish criminals, even with death. Civil authority is empowered by God to use its sword to execute wrongdoers.

But Romans 13 also seems to demand an unquestioning loyalty to the state that most American Christians would reject. "He who rebels against authority," we read in 13:2, "rebels against what God has instituted, and those who do so will bring God's judgment upon themselves." What about the American Revolution or the rebellions against Communist regimes that brought down the Soviet Union? Were these rebellions against God? If taken literally, Romans 13 claims too much authority for the state and calls upon Christians to tolerate too much injustice. The mere fact that the state can exercise the "sword" does not mean that it should always be deferred to or that it enjoys a moral right to execute human beings.

Nor is it clear the "sword" mentioned in Romans 13:4 refers to the executioner's blade. It is more likely that the "sword" here refers to the state's authority to use force to keep the peace, relying normally on police or soldiers and not on executioners. In this case Paul writes to discourage Christians from joining a tax rebellion, lest the policeman accompanying the government's toll and tax collectors use his sword. Most biblical scholars agree that Romans 13 does not offer an argument justifying capital punishment.

PASSAGES AGAINST CAPITAL PUNISHMENT

Cain, Moses, and David: Protections for Murderers

If God commands the execution of murderers in Genesis 9:6, why does the same God refuse to impose this penalty on Cain, Moses, or David? Cain slays his own brother in an act of premeditated murder; God punishes the Bible's first murderer severely, but not with death. Indeed, Genesis 4:15 reports that God puts a mark of protection on Cain so no one else will kill him. There is to be no blood vengeance for the death of Abel. In Exodus 2:11–12 Moses kills an Egyptian for striking a Hebrew, covers up his crime, and flees into the desert when he learns that the Pharaoh seeks to execute him. Decades later God takes this exiled murderer and transforms him into the liberator of the Hebrews. Instead of executing him, God makes Moses an instrument of saving justice. And in 2 Samuel 11–12:25 we read how King David takes the wife of his loyal captain, Uriah the Hittite, and then has Uriah murdered to cover up his own crimes. When the prophet Nathan traps David into facing his sin, David acknowledges that such a man as he has been *deserves* to die. But a merciful God does not call for David's execution, allowing him instead to repent and to continue to rule over Israel.

Sodom and Gomorrah and the Weeds and Wheat: Protections for the Innocent

In Genesis 18:20–33 God informs Abraham of the outcry raised against Sodom and Gomorrah and of a plan to investigate whether these cities deserve to be destroyed. But when challenged on this by Abraham, God concedes that it would be wrong to kill the just inhabitants along with the sinners, even if the number of the just within the Cities of the Plain turns out to be infinitesimal. So the Lord promises that Sodom will not be destroyed if there are but *ten* just persons found in the city. God's justice, then, does not sweep up the innocent with the guilty but protects the lives of the just. Capital punishment, as we will see, can make no such claim.

Matthew 13:24–30 expresses a similar concern for the lives of the innocent. In this parable of the weeds and the wheat, the weeds planted in a farmer's field represent "bad seed" mingled among the righteous and innocent. But when workers ask to remove these weeds (slaying the evil ones), they are told, "No, because when you pull out the weeds, you might pull up the wheat [i.e., the righteous] as well." Thomas Aquinas acknowledged that this passage *seems* to argue against capital punishment, but Aquinas himself believed the death penalty could be imposed without harming the innocent.[4] As we will see, the sad history of capital punishment shows how wrong Aquinas was.

Ezekiel, Isaiah, and Jonah: God's Preference for Repentance

Ezekiel and Isaiah tell us of a God who prefers repentance to the punishment of death. In Ezekiel 33:11 the God who would not slay Cain, Moses, or David tells the prophet, "As I live, I have no desire for the death of the wicked. I would rather that the wicked should mend their ways and live." And in Isaiah 55:7 the prophet tells Israel, "Let the scoundrel forsake his way, and the wicked man his thoughts; Let him turn to the Lord for mercy; to our God who is generous in forgiving."

Even God's critics know the Lord is compassionate and eager to forgive. Jonah finds this divine mercy galling when the reluctant prophet is sent to preach repentance to Nineveh. Preferring a God of wrath who calls down hellfire on his enemies, Jonah sulks when God forgives the repentant citizens of Nineveh: "I knew that you are a gracious and compassionate God, long suffering, ever-constant, always ready to relent and not inflict punishment."

Jesus and the Call to Forgiveness

For nearly two millennia Christian support for capital punishment has relied on one minor New Testament passage (Romans 13:1–7), overlooking or sidestepping the New Testament's central message of forgiveness. The forgiveness of sinners and the love of one's enemies lie at the heart of who Jesus is and who Christians possessing "the mind of Christ" are called to be. Even the most cursory reading of the gospels reveals a Jesus who preaches and practices a scandalous and prodigal mercy toward the worst possible sinners and who expects the same kind of compassion and forgiveness to characterize any who would follow after him.

Matthew 5:38–42 undoes any Christian support of capital punishment based on an eye for an eye. It sets a new standard for justice. Resistance to evil cannot be based on vengeance or mirror the violence of one's enemies. An eye for an eye has been replaced by turning one's cheek, and (in Matthew 5:43–48) hatred for one's enemies has been replaced by love and prayers for those who hate and persecute us. Jesus calls his followers to imitate the mercy of a God who "sends the rain on the innocent and the wicked."

Matthew 6:12–15 makes it clear that forgiveness is not optional for those who follow Jesus. In the only prayer Jesus ever taught his disciples, we ask that God will "forgive us our sins *as we forgive* those who sin against us." We pray the Lord's Prayer knowing that our *failure* to forgive will render us unfit for the Reign of God: "For if you forgive others the wrongs they have done, your heavenly Father will also forgive you; but if you do not forgive others, then your Father will not forgive the wrongs you have done."

Jesus and Capital Punishment

In John 7:53–8:11 Jesus is confronted directly with the question of capital punishment. A woman caught in the very act of adultery is dragged before him, and his opponents ask if he supports the Mosaic Law about stoning such sinners.

Since the scribes and Pharisees are using the woman to set a trap for Jesus, it is clear they expect him to oppose her execution. He does not disappoint them. "Let the one among you who is without sin be the first to throw a stone at her," he tells them. Traditionally, eyewitnesses were to cast the first stone, but here Jesus commands the woman's accusers turn their eyes inward, recognizing a sinfulness they share with the one they were ready to kill. Disarmed by this and unable to meet Jesus's new standard for execution, the mob disperses. Jesus is now alone with the guilty woman. "Has no one condemned you?" he asks her. She replies, "No one, sir." "Nor do I condemn you: go and sin no more."

Dozens of times in the Bible God's people are reminded that they too were once slaves and aliens in Egypt, and that they must therefore show the slave and the alien in their midst the same kind of compassion God showed to them. Here Jesus reminds his audience (and all Christians who read this text) that they too are sinners and that they must therefore treat other sinners with mercy as God has treated them. Casting stones at sinners is not an option for those who have seen the sin in their own hearts and who desire the mercy of God.

As Jesus's own execution approaches, he will not allow his followers to take up the sword against the angry mob bent on killing him. Violence only leads to more violence, he warns. And from the cross he asks God not to retaliate against his persecutors but rather to "forgive them, they know not what they do." It is hard to believe this Jesus approves of the death penalty.

The Crucifixion of Jesus should give any Christian pause about supporting the death penalty, for the Passion and death of Jesus form the tale of an innocent man wrongfully accused and unjustly executed—a story repeated far too many times in the tragic history of the death penalty. Christ's solidarity with all the innocent victims of capital punishment should make Christians uneasy about supporting any state-sanctioned killing.

Moral Arguments

Thomas Aquinas argued we could execute criminals like we slaughter beasts, "for . . . an evil man is worse than a beast, and more harmful"; these days letters to the editor often describe persons convicted of heinous crimes as "monsters."[5] Yet we know that murderers are still human beings, that Pope John Paul II was surely right when he wrote that "not even a murderer loses his personal dignity," and that capital punishment cannot be justified on the grounds that criminals are animals fit for slaughter.[6] That is not a Christian position.

Nor can we argue, as some ancients did, that the criminal is a gangrenous limb of the body politic that may be amputated for the common good. Individual persons are not merely an appendage of society, and we cannot intentionally and routinely execute them to serve some greater good. Only totalitarian regimes believe that individuals are but cogs of the larger whole.

DETERRENCE

Capital punishment proponents argue that the death penalty is justified because it provides one or all of the following deterrents: it prevents convicted murderers or criminals from committing further murders or crimes, it discourages other people from committing similar crimes, and it prevents victims or the public from taking vengeance into their own hands.

Putting someone to death will keep them from committing future crimes, just as amputating a thief's hands will end his career as a pickpocket. But that hardly proves that either form of punishment is justified. Studies show that "murderers are among those offenders least likely to repeat their crime even when released" and that murderers sentenced to life without parole are less than half as violent or dangerous as other prisoners.[7] One study of six hundred prisoners who were released from death row in the 1970s showed that only five killed again, while four were later exonerated. To prevent five additional homicides it would have been necessary to execute six hundred people, four of whom were proven innocent.

The idea that capital punishment discourages other people from committing murder or other serious crimes is ancient and unfounded. Again, Aquinas wrote that "when . . . punishment is made plain, namely death or other things terrifying to men, then . . . the punishment terrifies more than the sin attracts."[8] But as Gershwin wrote in *Porgy and Bess*,

"It ain't necessarily so." Former U.S. attorney general Janet Reno has commented that "I have inquired for most of my adult life about studies that might show that the death penalty is a deterrent. And I have not seen any research that would substantiate that point." Repeated United Nations studies on the link between the death penalty and homicide rates have found that it is unreasonable to believe that capital punishment deters murder even marginally more than does life imprisonment.[9]

Study after study has failed to show that capital punishment provides more effective deterrence than life imprisonment. States and nations that abolish the death penalty do *not* report increases in their murder or crime rates, whereas nations or states that impose the death penalty are unable to report corresponding declines in their murder rates.

If anything, studies indicate that capital punishment may actually *increase* rates of homicide in some communities. A *New York Times* survey in 2000 showed that that homicide rates in states using capital punishment have been 48 percent to 101 percent higher than in states without the death penalty. Likewise, recent studies in Oklahoma and California found significant increases in stranger killings and homicide rates after the death penalty was reinstated. A recent United Nations report indicates that among nations with very high homicide rates, five countries that still impose the death penalty average 41.6 murders per 100,000 people; in contrast to this, five others that have now dispensed with the death penalty average just 21.6 murders for every 100,000 people.[10]

Most law enforcement officials understand that capital punishment is not a deterrent. Studies have shown that fewer than 2 percent of police chiefs in this country see capital punishment as an effective deterrent to violent crime, whereas more than two-thirds doubt the death penalty has any real impact on homicide rates. Robert M. Morgenthau, who has served as district attorney for Manhattan for three decades, offered this judgment of capital punishment and deterrence: "Take it from someone who has spent a career in federal and state law enforcement, enacting the death penalty...would be a grave mistake. Prosecutors must reveal the dirty little secret they too often share only among themselves: The death penalty actually hinders the fight against crime."

Proponents of the death penalty like to argue that capital punishment *could* be an effective deterrent if its application were more certain and swift. They point out that the vast majority of murderers are not in fact sentenced to death and that extensive appeals and delays can postpone executions for years if not decades.

But should we remedy this situation by swiftly executing most murderers or by removing the appeals process? There were over sixteen thousand homicides in the United States in 2002. Executing most of the people responsible for these killings would require a *hundredfold* increase in the annual number of executions. Likewise, softening or curtailing appeals would only increase the already frightening number of *wrongful* executions. Between 43 and 68 percent of death penalty cases are overturned on appeal, and since 1973 there have been 118 persons released from death row because they were later found to be innocent. Greasing the wheels of justice will only lead to the death of more innocents.

If capital punishment reduces violence by discouraging victims' families and the public from taking vengeance into their own hands, why do studies show that the death penalty does not reduce the murder rate and may even contribute to a rise in the number of homicides? For centuries we executed people in public because this spectacle was supposed to deter crime, but some recent studies show a spike in murder and violent crime rates following well-publicized executions. The reason may be simple. As the U.S. Conference of Catholic Bishops and a chorus of other Christian leaders have argued, "We cannot teach that killing is wrong by killing." Instead of slaking the passion for violence, the death penalty inflames this passion and teaches that the cure to violence is more violence.

RETRIBUTION

Death penalty proponents argue that capital punishment is a fit retribution for the crime of murder and that by taking the life of the murderer the state redresses the injustice of the original crime, balancing the scales of justice, and affirms the sanctity of human life.

Clearly, punishment does have a retributive function. Pope John Paul II, who called the death penalty "both cruel and unnecessary," acknowledged in *Evangelium Vitae* that "the primary purpose of the punishment which society inflicts is 'to redress the disorder caused by the offense.'" But the pope also believed that punishment should not be reduced to "mere retribution" or to some form of "social retaliation" or "institutional vengeance."

Christian proponents of a retributive justice that calls for taking the life of killers face two initial problems, both already mentioned. In the Sermon on the Mount Jesus radically reforms the notion of retribution for Christians and excludes retaliation that mirrors the violence of the criminal. An eye for an eye cannot, for Christians, justify taking a life for a life. And in modern (and civilized) society Christians, like most of their fellow citizens, have abandoned corporal punishment as a criminal penalty. We do not support inflicting a burn for a burn or a stripe for a stripe. So how can a strict rule of retribution justify capital punishment's ultimate assault on the human body?

For centuries Christians have declared themselves unwilling to go to war unless it was truly a last resort—that is, unless there were no other alternatives. Christian churches calling for abolition argue that the same rule applies to capital punishment. Putting a person to death is an extraordinary act of violence, a premeditated assault that cannot be justified by the mere need to retaliate for another violent act. If there is *any* other option, *any* less violent, brutal, or savage means to redress a crime without replicating the original violence, that other option must be used.

Taking a life for a life does not "redress the disorder caused by the offense"; it only mirrors and replicates it. Murder cannot be undone, and killing murderers does not return victims to life or to their families. Indeed, if we are to carry out executions in ways that even minimally protect the innocent from being put to death by allowing extended appeals, then maintaining capital punishment actually ends up protracting the suffering of victims' families for decades.

Nor does taking a life "teach" the sanctity of life, particularly when there is any other option. It teaches the sanctity of violence. A government that imposes the death penalty as retribution when it has viable alternatives teaches its citizens to rely on violence as a solution to problems.

INNOCENCE

Christians know full well that innocent people are put to death by the government. The Roman Empire executed Jesus, Peter, Paul, and a slew of other early Christians. From the martyr Stephen to Bishop Oscar Romero, the litany of Christian saints is replete with the names of innocent persons put to death in the name of church or state.

The actual number of people executed each year in China may be as high as ten thousand. Certainly there is good reason to doubt all of them were guilty or justly convicted. And what of the hundreds executed each year in Iran or Vietnam? Were there not ten innocent men and women among all these dead?

George W. Bush confidently proclaims there were *no* innocent persons among the 152 people executed while he was governor of Texas. But the year Bush was elected to the White House, Governor George Ryan of Illinois announced that 13 death row prisoners in that state had been wrongfully convicted since 1977. A Stanford study reports that at least 23 innocent persons were executed in the United States between 1900 and 1987, and the National Coalition to Abolish the Death Penalty reports 8 more cases since 1987. As we saw above, 118 death row inmates have been exonerated in the United States since 1973.

The killing of innocent persons is sometimes a tragic necessity. But when the state has alternatives that can provide an equal or superior deterrent and that can adequately protect the community from further crime or violence, there can be no justification for state-sanctioned taking of innocent life.

DISPARATE RACIAL OUTCOMES

In 1987 the Supreme Court admitted in *McClesky v. Kemp* that there was a "discrepancy" in the imposition of death sentences "that appears to correlate with race." The court did not remedy this discrepancy because, it said, such "disparities in sentencing are an inevitable part of our criminal justice system." A 1990 U.S. General Accounting Office report also found "a pattern of evidence indicating racial disparities in the charging, sentencing, and imposition of the death penalty," and a recent Justice Department review of the federal death penalty found numerous racial disparities.

African Americans make up about 12 percent of the population but account for 42 percent of current death row inmates. The homicide rate (like the poverty and unemployment rates) is higher among blacks than whites, but a Philadelphia study comparing similar cases showed that African American defendants were nearly *four times as likely* to receive the death penalty.

Racial bias in sentencing shows up primarily in relation to race of the victims. Since 1977 there have been just about as many blacks killed in this country as whites, but 84 percent of the people put to death were convicted of murdering *white* victims. In Florida, Illinois, Oklahoma, North Carolina, and Mississippi those who kill whites are four to five times more likely to receive the death penalty.

The death penalty also discriminates against the poor. As a former warden of San Quentin Prison once noted, "capital punishment is a privilege of the poor." Studies repeatedly show that good legal representation is the most important factor in avoiding a death sentence, and that that 90 percent of those sitting on death row could not afford such representation because they were indigent at the time of their arrest.

Christians are called to make a preferential option for the poor and to stand with the marginalized and powerless. Capital punishment amounts to punishment for those without capital, and thus it violates our obligation to protect the poor from discrimination.

COSTS

States do not save money by putting people to death. Studies in California, Kansas, Maryland, North Carolina, Florida, and New York have shown that capital punishment is far more expensive than keeping someone in prison for life. Different studies put the cost of putting someone to death at $3 to $7 million—at least six times more than the cost of a sentence of life without parole. Most of these costs would not be eliminated by cutting off the appeals process, since the bulk of the tab for putting someone to death is run up before and during the initial conviction and sentencing phases of the trial.

Money spent on capital punishment means less money to fight crime or run schools and hospitals. New Jersey spent $16 million in 1991 to impose the death penalty; it then fired five hundred police officers the next year to balance the budget. When New York State reinstated the death penalty in 1995, its corrections department estimated that reinstatement would cost an additional $118 million a year. This happened even as the legislature was making dramatic cuts in funding for education and health care.

And money is not the only price we pay for capital punishment. The United States has become a pariah in the international community thanks to our unwillingness to abandon the death penalty. Other nations will not honor our extradition treaties unless we promise not to execute, and groups like Amnesty International condemn our abysmal human rights record. Instead of standing with our European allies and a growing majority of the world's nations, America finds itself in the same club with China, Iran, and Vietnam, the planet's other leading executioners.

A CRUEL AND UNUSUAL PRACTICE

From a global and religious perspective, the once-universal practice of capital punishment has become increasingly "unusual," no doubt due to what Chief Justice Earl Warren once called "the evolving standards of decency that mark the progress of a maturing society." A growing majority of the world's nations and churches now call the death penalty morally abhorrent. These nations and religious bodies have cast the executioner's ax into the dustbin of history.

The cruelty of most traditional forms of capital punishment is too obvious to rehearse here. Not surprising, since cruelty and terror were long the point of executions. But even modern and so-called humane forms of the death penalty remain cruel. There are ample horror stories about prolonged and ghastly electrocutions, nor is it clear that those put to death by lethal injection do not suffer after they have been paralyzed.

But the real cruelty of the modern death penalty in America is the decades spent waiting to be executed: knowing the manner and fashion in which one will be put to death, watching and waiting as the date grows ever closer, and watching the prisoners in the line ahead of you become "dead men walking" to their grave. This cruelty explains why so many of those slated for execution stop submitting appeals, wishing only to end the torture of their long, horrible sojourn in death's waiting room.

The death penalty is hardly less cruel to the families of murder victims. They must endure death penalty trials that often last four times as long as trials for other murderers. This means they must revisit their suffering through years and sometimes through decades of appeals; it means they must relive their original trauma yet again at the time of execution. Many of these family members are further wounded when a long-delayed execution fails to provide them with the peace or closure they had so desperately awaited and that society had so insistently promised.

Forward in Discernment, Forward in Faith

There has been a sea change in the Christian stance on capital punishment, with the vast majority of mainline denominations now joining the great majority of the earth's nations in moral opposition to a once-universal practice. Church leaders and theologians have turned against the death penalty because it is inconsistent with Christ's call to forgiveness; because it weakens, not strengthens, our commitment to the sanctity of life; because it adds to, not diminishes, the culture of death and the cycle of violence; because it discriminates against the poor and against people of color; and because it takes human life unnecessarily. We should give thanks that American Christians at long last are rejecting the executioner's ax as we earlier rejected the overseer's whip and the torturer's tongs. Our progress has been halting, but that makes it no less recognizably real.

Notes

1. Michael L. Westmoreland-White and Glen Stassen, "Biblical Perspectives on the Death Penalty," in *Religion and the Death Penalty: A Call for Reckoning*, edited by Erik C. Owens, John D. Carlson, and Eric P. Elshtain (Grand Rapids, MI: Eerdmans, 2004), 124.

2. David Novak, "Can Capital Punishment Ever Be Justified in the Jewish Tradition?" in Owens, Carlson, and Elshtain, *Religion and the Death Penalty*, 35–41.

3. E. Christian Brugger, *Capital Punishment and Roman Catholic Moral Tradition* (Notre Dame, IN: University of Notre Dame Press, 2003), 75–84.

4. Thomas Aquinas, *Summa Theologiae*, II-II, 64, 2.

5. Ibid.

6. John Paul II, *Evangelium Vitae*, 9.

7. Gardner C. Hanks, *Against the Death Penalty: Christian and Secular Arguments against Capital Punishment* (Scottdale, PA: Herald Press, 1997), 85–89.

8. Thomas Aquinas, *Summa Theologiae*, II-II, 108, 3.

9. Roger Hood, *The Death Penalty: A World-Wide Perspective* (Oxford: Clarendon Press, 2002), 230.

10. A good deal of this information may be obtained by visiting the Web sites of Amnesty International and the National Coalition to Abolish the Death Penalty.

Honoring Those Who Work

ALEXIA SALVATIERRA

There will be no poor among you.

—*Deuteronomy* 15:4

The hotel housekeepers standing against the wall were all crying. It was December 15, 2002, the culmination of three years of intense struggle with the management of Loews Santa Monica Luxury Beach Hotel. The housekeepers were gathered, along with the top management of the hotel, ten local clergy, local press, politicians, and union leaders to celebrate management's agreement to take a neutral stance on the issue of union representation. With union representation would come the possibility of a contract guaranteeing a living wage, health insurance, a voice in the daily decisions that impacted their lives. The housekeepers' tears were tears of almost incredulous joy. Rosa summed up the feelings of her companions with eloquent simplicity: "Now I can imagine being able to take good care of my family; maybe my children will even be able to go to college!"

For the Loews workers, this was a Jubilee moment. The biblical concept of Jubilee is rooted in the mandate of Leviticus 25. Every fifty years, the people of Israel were expected to "proclaim liberty throughout the land" by canceling debts, freeing slaves, and redistributing land equitably. If the Jubilee injunctions were followed, true liberty would ensue and the land itself would be blessed. For the Loews workers on December 15, the moment had arrived in which their daily experience of bone-crunching poverty might finally be over. Jubilee had become a real and tangible possibility.

The story of the Loews workers is both history and parable. Their plight, their struggle, and their ultimate victory reveal the nature of our societal crossroads and the core of our hope. The role of people of faith in the Loews workers' story offers a lesson in the central calling of this hour for those who follow the Carpenter King.

Making Bricks without Straw: What Working Poverty Means Today

In 1999, hotel housekeepers at Loews earned an average of $7 per hour to clean rooms that cost $450 per night. Many traveled over an hour on the bus to get to work because they could not afford beach-area rents. Even the apartments that they rented in the poorest areas of the city cost an average of $750 per month. The hotel industry employs one of the highest percentages of single mothers; the majority of the single mothers cleaning Loews' hotel rooms brought in so little money that they were eligible for food stamps. Many workers also were forced to rely on MediCal or public health clinics for their families' medical needs because of their lack of access to affordable employer-provided health insurance.

The situation of the Loews workers was far from unique. According to a recent study by the Los Angeles Alliance for a New Economy, over 30 percent of the families in Los Angeles County can be classified as working poor. This means that at least one adult in the family is employed, but the overall income of the family remains insufficient to cover basic expenses. A worker earning $7 per hour brings home approximately $960 per month; in 2004, the average cost of a two-bedroom apartment in the city of Los Angeles was $1,350 per month.

The number of working poor families has increased steadily over the past twenty years and now rises exponentially. Why? Part of the answer reflects a winner-take-all ethic. In the year 1970, the average CEO earned thirty times more than his lowest-paid worker; in 2000, he earned three hundred times more. In 2005, according to *Fortune Magazine,* he earned over four hundred times more. In the past, the corporate code of values included providing for the basic well-being of employees and the general welfare of the community and not simply earning a healthy profit. Now Wal-Mart leads a "race to the bottom" in which economic winners maximize profit by cutting costs and bleeding communities. Of course, someone else must pick up those costs, and that someone else is often the taxpayers. While the State of California struggles with a fiscal crisis, over one hundred thousand Wal-Mart employees depend on MediCal to provide for their basic health needs.

Loews Santa Monica Luxury Beach Hotel also benefited from tax subsidies. It is located in a special "tourist zone"—an area in which the City of Santa Monica had invested over $180 million to attract tourism. The city had declared a moratorium on further development of luxury hotels in the zone, thus creating an economic bonanza for the existing hotels. When thirty hotel employees began in 1999 to organize a drive for union representation, they believed that Loews was making sufficient profits to be able to pay a living wage and provide health benefits. Unfortunately, management did not agree.

Indispensable Partners in Struggle

In the city of Los Angeles, workers with union representation earn an average of 20 percent more than nonunion workers; a majority of union workers also still enjoy affordable employer-provided health insurance. In contrast, over 60 percent of the working poor in Los Angeles County lack employer-provided heath insurance.

The employer-driven "race to the bottom" explains why it has become so difficult for workers to obtain representation and good contracts. Human Rights Watch reports that in 1999 over thirty thousand workers were found by the National Labor Relations Board to have been fired or otherwise penalized because they were supporting a union-organizing drive or contract fight in their workplace. But this figure represents only a small portion of the workers who pay a price for their union activity. These days hundreds of law firms specialize in coaching corporations on how to defeat organizing efforts by intimidating, suspending, or firing union leaders. Winning a Labor Board determination of unfair labor practices requires *years* of court appearances.

Even a favorable board decision provides back pay only for the amount of time that the plaintiff was not employed at any job and had no government help—and how long can a low-wage single mother go without any job or government help? Nearly all the pundits who write each Labor Day about the "dying" U.S. labor movement fail to mention these systematic efforts to murder it, nor do they mention how a movement so marked for death somehow refuses to die.

After Loews workers in Santa Monica began to organize, Loews hired a union-busting law firm that specializes in convincing employees not to choose union representation. Management proceeded to carry out a variety of strategies designed to intimidate, harass, or bribe workers into abandoning their quest for union representation. At one point in the struggle, five worker leaders were fired in a three-month period.

Given the tools available to management in such struggles, it is clear that the voice and power of the workers must be combined with the voice and power of customers and citizens in order for the workers to have a chance of success. Fortunately, the Loews workers were not alone in their David vs. Goliath struggle. Santa Monica's activist community organized its own response to the workers' plight. SMART (the Santa Monica Alliance for Responsible Tourism) brought residents together in support of policies that would force publicly subsidized luxury hotels to take greater responsibility for the well-being of workers. But the hotels fought back: in the fall of 2000 they promoted a spurious "Living Wage" initiative that would have provided living wages to a handful of city employees and quietly prevented the city council from ever passing any stronger or more inclusive living-wage legislation. The corporations spent over $2 million, but their phony initiative was overwhelmingly defeated. Still they would not give up: once a broad living-wage ordinance was finally enacted in the summer of 2001, the hotels came back with a *new* initiative to repeal the new ordinance. Despite these shenanigans, SMART's endless, creative, and passionate community support was a core factor in the Loews workers' ultimate victory.

The Special Role of People of Faith

A core component of the Santa Monica public policy and Loews workers' victories was the involvement of CLUE (Clergy and Laity United for Economic Justice). CLUE is a network of religious leaders and congregations from all faith traditions who support low-wage workers in their struggles to attain living wages, access to health care, respect in the workplace, and the right to organize. CLUE brings unique gifts to the broad community-worker coalition's struggle for economic justice.

MORAL AUTHORITY

The first gift that religious leaders and communities bring is moral authority. The religious community does not represent workers' interests. Congregations include workers *and* "bosses"—persons from all points in the political spectrum. Often the congregation's immediate interests lie with the owners and managers whose financial contributions are vital to institutional survival. Thus, when a religious community speaks for workers, there is no doubt that it is speaking—courageously—for justice. This also means that when corporate or political decision makers hear such a message, they cannot easily dismiss it and may even prove capable of being influenced by it.

One of the more dramatic examples of the power of moral authority occurred during the 2004 Southern California grocery store workers' strike and lockout. Three months into the strike, the CEO of Vons/Safeway/Pavilions—Steven Burd—declared that he was not coming back to the negotiating table under any circumstances. Had Burd's final offer prevailed, it would have meant the loss of health insurance for many of the seventy thousand affected workers and poverty-level salary caps for newly hired workers. But CLUE learned that Burd had recently become a devout evangelical Christian. And so in January 2004 CLUE organized a two-day statewide pilgrimage involving over two hundred workers and congregational leaders to Burd's northern California home. CLUE also delivered ten thousand postcards addressed to Burd as well as resolutions/statements/letters from top religious authorities from every major denomination and tradition. The pilgrimage attracted major press coverage. As a result of the public pressure, CLUE leaders were able to meet privately with the pastors of Burd's new congregation and urge them to appeal to Burd to return to the bargaining table until a fair settlement was reached. Two weeks later, Burd did in fact return. He stayed for fifteen days, until a new contract—one far from ideal but better than any previous offer—was negotiated.

Religious leaders can use moral authority not only to advocate for workers but also to break down barriers to community involvement in workers' battles and open the lines of communication for the voices of workers to reach the general public. When the luxury hotels in Santa Monica attempted in 2001 to enact their spurious living-wage ordinance, the community was confused at first about whom to believe. Religious leaders' trusted testimony gave credibility to the workers and their allies. "Clergy street theater" brought press attention to the truth about the initiative. At one point, clergy distributed tiny pieces of pie to the customers at the local farmers' market against the backdrop of a pie chart showing the small percentage of luxury hotel profits that were being spent on workers' salaries.

ANCIENT INSPIRATION AND ENCOURAGEMENT

The second gift that religious leaders and communities bring is a set of ancient tools for inspiration and encouragement. José was a worker leader in a fight for union representation at a hotel. When his best friend was fired for supporting the campaign, José was terrified. His six children depended on his salary, and he had been through persecution and trauma in his native country before receiving political asylum in the United States. He went to his priest for advice. Fortunately, this priest was affiliated with CLUE. He told José not to be afraid. He said that God was a God of justice—and that Moses was the first union organizer. After this, José realized that if he lost his job because he was doing the will of God he would surely find another. Now he wanted his children to share some of this fearlessness and also to realize that they were just as much children of God and just as deserving of the good things of life as any other children. When José returned to the struggle, full of inspiration, his coworkers were deeply impressed. They knew how much he had to lose, and his courage inspired their dedication. The workers won their battle.

The pastoral and human rights skills of religious leaders have made a crucial difference in workers' capacity to sustain their involvement and commitment when they have been harassed, threatened, and punished for their organizing activities. When 250 union workers at the Wyndham LAX hotel were fired in 2001, they were so demoralized that initial efforts by union organizers to fight back were ineffective. CLUE leaders began to visit workers individually and attend worker committee meetings. Out of these meetings emerged new strategies, such as monthly vigils outside the hotel where every fired worker was named and lifted up in prayer. The pastoral nature of this work attracted clergy and lay leaders who had never seen themselves as activists before. After each vigil, management hired back more former workers. Ultimately, the company agreed to neutrality on union representation; it also gave the original workers preferential rehiring.

TOOLS TO AWAKEN THE SLEEPING GIANT OF CONGREGATIONAL POWER

The third gift that religious leaders bring is a capacity to awake the sleeping giant that is the religious congregation itself.

Most Americans do not think of themselves as activists. Even more to the point, they don't perceive themselves as having the time or resources to *become* activists. Increasing workloads and diminishing support networks crimp opportunities for activism. On the other hand, nine out of ten Americans assert that they believe in God. This means that congregations provide one of the few remaining potential bridges to community activism for millions of the faithful.

In recent decades the religious Right has been extraordinarily successful in mobilizing congregational power for political purposes. What makes this achievement extraordinary is that they have been able to do it with virtually no scriptural warrant. For example, while only half a dozen passages in the whole of the Jewish and Christian scriptures deal with what we moderns would call homosexual behavior, the Bible contains at least six hundred passages in which God insists that economic justice and fairness to workers mark the essence not just of right relations among humans but of right worship itself. It is no exaggeration to say that God is properly "introduced" in the Bible as one who hears the moaning of those held in oppressive Egyptian bondage. It is likewise no exaggeration to say that any preacher who takes the Bible seriously and who preaches it seriously will be involved in some degree of congregational awakening.

Perhaps the most striking example of the power of the awakened giant is the defeat of Wal-Mart's plans to build one of its "SuperCenters" in Inglewood, California. Wal-Mart is the widely acknowledged international leader of the race to the bottom. Most Wal-Mart employees receive some kind of government subsidy in order to survive, and for every two low-wage jobs that Wal-Mart creates, three comparatively good ones are wiped out. Wal-Mart had never lost a battle to build a new SuperCenter in a low-income community until April 2004. LAANE (the Los Angeles Alliance for a New Economy) and CLUE worked together to organize the Coalition for a Better Inglewood; the coalition in turn organized Inglewood's primarily black and Hispanic residents to defeat Wal-Mart's ballot initiative, which would have overruled city council mandates and eliminated community oversight measures in relation to the proposed new SuperCenter. CLUE secured the active involvement of over forty leading Christian and Muslim African American clergy. These clergy then involved their congregations in stepping out to vote against the initiative. The push from the pulpit during the weekend before the final vote reached an estimated fifteen thousand people.

Implications for Our Common Future

The Loews workers experienced a Jubilee moment. Other workers involved in the community-labor-religious coalition in Los Angeles and in other parts of the country have experienced similar moments of real hope for freedom from the desperation of poverty. The role of the religious community in creating these Jubilee experiences is rich, vital, and connected to the deepest roots of our faith traditions. This role attracts religious leaders and congregations across a broad theological spectrum. As long as the common focus is on economic justice for the working poor, conservative evangelical Christians join hands with liberal reform Jews; African American Baptists work with LGBT leaders from the Metropolitan Community Churches. There are huge implications in this phenomenon for the future of progressive religion in our society.

In December of 2004 CLUE representatives participated in a national gathering of progressive religious leaders that had been convened for a serious examination of the causes of the overwhelming Christian vote for a conservative president. The leaders who gathered recognized that there has been nothing preordained about the devolution from an ascendant prophetic voice in the days of Rev. Martin Luther King, Jr., to the shrill moralism of today's most prominent Christian voices. A strategic triad, joining the religious Right to the political Right and corporate Right, has prevailed in the course of a thirty-year assault on progressive elements and values. Each partner in the triad played a specific and indispensable role. When religious communities were unable to participate directly in partisan politics, their support of conservative public policy initiatives was timed to coincide with corporate and political support of candidates who could carry the initiatives to victory.

People of faith focused on economic justice have the potential to help create a parallel triad, working in concert with the anticorporate Left (primarily the labor movement) and with the reconstituted progressive political movement represented by MoveOn.org. But this new triad cannot emerge without a comparable thirty-year effort, which in turn will require the active involvement of young religious leaders in the process. And herein lies a challenge.

Postelection studies showed that mainline Protestants were the only religious voters who increased their allegiance to a progressive agenda from 2000 to 2004. That's the good news. The bad news is that the average age of mainline Protestants today is around fifty-five, and the mainline share of the country's population has now entered free fall. Some sociologists of religion already refer to mainline bodies as "the historic Protestant churches," indicating the extent of mainline evaporation. Younger Christians today are increasingly found in evangelical churches, which in turn tend to support conservative agendas and candidates.

Across the country, however, many evangelical Christians are now demonstrating an increasing concern for the poor and are questioning social and political agendas that ignore the plight of the needy. In Los Angeles CLUE has responded to this increasing interest by actively recruiting evangelical interns to work on economic justice campaigns. When these interns fight side by side with low-wage workers and congregational leaders from different faith traditions to hold multinational corporations accountable or to pass worker-friendly public policies, their worldviews and affiliations often change dramatically. Young religious leaders whose consciousness is formed by the experience of working with low-wage workers and with passionately committed congregational leaders could play a pivotal role within a broader movement to revitalize progressive discourse and transform the politics of the twenty-first century.

Learning to Love Luther in the Struggle against Oppression

Each leader in the worker justice movement has a personal way of construing its spiritual foundation. Instead of trying to give a comprehensive picture of the role that faith traditions play in this movement, I would like to share the religious wellsprings of my own involvement over many years as an ordained pastor of the Evangelical Lutheran Church in America (ELCA).

Like everyone, I cannot read the Bible without being struck by the insistence of the Hebrew prophets on just economic relations. Their call is comprehensive, incorporating demands that impact trade relations, worker-management issues, and the right to wealth. Their call and their critique even include those who do not exercise direct power over economic decisions. The prophet Amos condemns the women of Israel's upper class, who had no practical role in the economic sphere, as "cows of Bashan . . . who will be taken away with hooks" for simply enjoying the fruits of others' labor and being indifferent to their plight.

In an echo of Amos's response to the cows of Bashan, Jesus tells the story of the rich man and Lazarus (Luke 16). The rich man is not portrayed as committing any active oppression of the poor. He is simply indifferent to the beggar who lives outside his front door. This alone causes him to be condemned to watch the beggar repose in Abraham's bosom for eternity while he himself suffers an eternity of the torments of hell. The implications are sobering, as they are meant to be.

My own Lutheran tradition may appear to be far removed from the plangent cries for justice of Jesus and the prophets. No one would say that economic justice was one of Martin Luther's primary passions, nor has Lutheranism been at the forefront of the fight for economic justice. But at the core of Lutheran theology there remains a call to faith in a God whose love is unimaginably great, broad, deep, and full. God's love embraces all aspects of our physical and emotional lives. God intends that we have "everything required to satisfy our bodily needs, such as food and clothing, house and home, fields and flocks, money and property." Martin Luther saw in our human labor a holy act when performed in faith and gratitude; in Luther's view "picking up a piece of straw" could be equal in God's eyes to formal prayer and study *(Treatise on Good Works)*.

While Luther may have emphasized the individual's existential relationship with God as the primary issue for faith, he unquestionably expected a lively faith to issue in righteous action. In both his small and large catechisms, he painted a passionate picture of the kinds of behavior that would arise from faith—including the arena of labor relations. For example, Luther's exegesis of the seventh commandment includes the following remarkable passage:

> For to steal is nothing else than to get possession of another's property wrongfully, which briefly comprehends all kinds of advantage in all sorts of trade to the disadvantage of our neighbor. To steal is to signify not only to empty our neighbor's coffer and pockets, but to be grasping in the market wherever there is trading or taking and giving of money for merchandise or labor. Therefore they are also called swivel-chair robbers, land- and highway-robbers, not pick-locks and sneak-thieves who snatch away the ready cash, but who sit on the chair [at home] and are styled great noblemen, and honorable, pious citizens, and yet rob and steal under a good pretext.
>
> No more shall all the rest prosper who change the open free market into a carrion-pit of extortion and a den of robbery, where the poor are daily overcharged, new burdens and high prices are imposed, and every one uses the market according to his caprice, and is even defiant and brags as though it were his fair privilege and right to sell his goods for as high a price as he please, and no one had a right to say a word against it.

Luther here takes the perspective of an independent producer whose experience of being robbed by the powerful consists of price gouging. But his critique applies with even more force to modern multinational corporations that seek profit at the expense of people not primarily by raising prices but rather by lowering wages. The core violation of "using the market according to his caprice as though it were his fair privilege and right" is as characteristic of Wal-Mart as it was of the powerful nobles of Luther's time.

Luther believes that it is the job of political decision makers to protect the economic interests of their constituency. As he writes in the same commentary: "to check such open wantonness there is need of the princes and government, who themselves would have eyes and the courage to establish and maintain order in all manner of trade and commerce, lest the poor be burdened and oppressed nor they themselves be loaded with other men's sins."

In a political democracy, we citizens are "the princes and government"; all of us now must possess "eyes and the courage to establish and maintain" basic fairness in trade and commerce. When we campaign for living-wage legislation or place conditions on Big Box retail development, we seek to ensure an economic order that does not allow the poor to be burdened and oppressed.

There Will Be No Poor Among You

Twenty years ago, a top official in the World Council of Churches said that we would be facing a growing contradiction between expanding political democracy and increasing economic tyranny—and that the resulting schizophrenic experience would produce profound anxiety. We are at the crossroads that he predicted. The anxiety that we all feel can lead us to seek demagogues who offer simple answers and a false sense of security. It can also lead us to build a movement that will address its source. Bad religion only masks the anxiety, whereas good religion exposes it and points toward resolution. The importance of renewed leadership by people of faith in resolving our general and nameless anxiety in the direction of justice cannot be overstated. It is the calling of the hour, of this *kairos* moment, for those who would follow in the steps of the Carpenter King.

Whom God Hath Joined Together

BILL SINKFORD

Where you go, I will go; where you lodge, I will lodge;
your people shall be my people, and your God my God.
Where you die I will die—there I will be buried.

—*Ruth* 1:16

"Whom God hath joined": these words from the traditional Protestant marriage ceremony are familiar to almost everyone. Marriages are often celebrated in churches and synagogues, in mosques and temples. Ministers, priests, and imams officiate at wedding ceremonies, calling their communities to celebrate the coming together of two people in love and commitment. In this respect marriage is a religious institution. And in this respect the rules of different religions determine who can marry and whether and on what grounds married persons can divorce. An obvious consequence is that the shape of religious marriage varies considerably from one faith community to another.

But marriages are also celebrated in courthouses; justices of the peace send millions of couples off into married life with calm efficiency. But whether it is a priest or a JP who actually does the deed, marriage is crucially a civil institution. The ceremonies might vary, and religious ceremonies might imply extra rules and prescriptions, but the enforceable laws—the civil laws—that govern all marriages do not vary.

It should not surprise us that this gets confused or that many people assume that the religious laws and religious values invoked in a wedding ceremony are decisive. After all, the officiating religious leader gets to say "By the power vested in me . . ." toward the climax of the service. But when that religious officiant signs the marriage license, it is a *civil* marriage license that she or he signs. In signing it, that religious leader is acting as an agent of the state. The clergy person is transforming the religious marriage he or she just solemnized into a *civil* marriage that is thereafter governed by the rules of the state.

We confuse religious and civil marriage at our peril. The danger is that we will enshrine one religious point of view in laws intended to govern and protect us all. That danger is more acute than ever because the United States has become the most religiously pluralistic society the earth has ever known. Americans today are not only Methodists but Mormons and Muslims and Sikhs; not only Baptists but Buddhists, Baha'is, Jains, and Jews; not only believers but agnostics and atheists. Additionally, about a quarter of all Americans declare themselves to be "unchurched."

The Christian Right argues that we are, or were meant to be, a Christian nation. If that were so, which of the many and varied Christian doctrines would we choose to be the ones governing civil law? The Roman Catholic Church is not only the largest Christian body, but, with some 67 million members, is the largest faith community of any kind in the United States. Catholic teaching does not permit divorce; nonetheless, millions of persons raised in the Catholic faith have sought and received civil divorces when their marriages became unsustainable. They could do this because civil marriage is governed not by religious laws but by civil laws. Should civil divorce be outlawed because the precepts of the Catholic Church reject divorce? Few would say yes to such a change.

What about marriage for same-sex couples? Many religious communities disapprove of it. Does that mean the state cannot make it legal? Declaring this area absolutely off-limits forfeits the civil society's power to fashion laws that promote the general welfare and provide the greatest good for the greatest number.

Everyone knows that the definition of civil marriage has become *the* hot-button issue in the culture war currently raging between the Christian Right and progressive forces in this country. On one side, the marriage-equality movement is pushing for the legalization of same-sex civil marriage and the extension of full civil benefits and protections to gay and lesbian families. On the other side, proponents of "traditional family values" warn of dire consequences if traditional definitions of marriage are changed by statute. They are doing everything they can to stop it: eleven states adopted so-called Defense of Marriage (DOMA) statutes in the last election. President Bush and his allies in Congress are pushing for a constitutional amendment to ban same-sex marriage.

In May of 2004, this issue exploded in Massachusetts. The previous fall, the state's highest court had found no compelling reason to deny same-sex couples the rights and responsibilities of civil marriage. In response, the state legislature took up an amendment to the state constitution that would define marriage as only between one man and one woman. Demonstrators on both sides of the issue lined Beacon Street in front of the golden-domed Massachusetts State House.

The national headquarters of the Unitarian Universalist Association happen to be located right next door to the State House. As a faith community, we had a decision to make. We could either be quiet or we could express our values. We decided to be articulate: we hung a sixteen- by twenty-foot banner on our building, facing the State House, reading: "Civil Marriage is a Civil Right." This ensured that state legislators, looking out their windows when they were in session, would see our message. And many of us stood out on Beacon Street as well. We stood there not in angry protest but as people of faith who believed that the religious and the civil institutions of marriage should not be confused—and that our government should take seriously its charge to be evenhanded, favoring no religion or religious view over another.

This not just an issue about constitutional rights; marriage equality touches the lives of real people. On May 17, 2004, I had the privilege of marrying Hillary and Julie Goodridge in the chapel of our Beacon Street headquarters. Hillary and Julie have been committed to one another now for eighteen years. They have for eighteen years cared for one another in sickness and in health. They are mothers to a wonderful daughter, Annie. They take her to soccer games; they attend PTA meetings. They love one another and threaten no one. All they wanted was for their relationship to be recognized as a legal marriage. Hillary and Julie were the lead named plaintiffs in the court case that finally made same-sex marriage legal in Massachusetts.

Without that legal status, more than a thousand legal rights had been denied to Hillary, Julie, and Annie at the federal level, and many more under Massachusetts law: these include tax benefits, health insurance benefits, the right to hospital visitation and to make medical decisions for one another, inheritance and Social Security benefits, family-leave benefits, rules that would protect both partners' interests if the relationship were to end, housing and immigration benefits, and hundreds more. Even with meticulous planning and the payment of hefty legal fees, Hillary and Julie would never have been able to replicate these rights no matter how many proxies and papers they signed. In the words of author and activist E. J. Graff in *What Is Marriage For?* "The difference between powers of attorney—or domestic partnership, for that matter—and marriage is the difference between a skateboard and a jet."

Just under the surface of the debate about marriage equality lie fundamental questions. What is marriage for? What is a family? The answers to these questions have been evolving for centuries—and never without generating controversy.

Families have functioned as economic entities—as units of production (think of the family farm) and a means of controlling property and wealth. Families have also been social and cultural entities: they have for thousands of years been the nexus where children are raised and socialized. Families are so different from culture to culture that in 1974, when the United Nations proclaimed the International Year of the Family, the organizing committee began by acknowledging not just that no one definition of "family" works across cultures but also that, in point of fact, "*the* family does not exist."

So what is a family? Clearly, it depends on whom you ask. But for more than two thousand years, religious communities have seen families as a microcosm and fundamental life-form within their particular faith tradition. The family is thus an institution freighted with an awful lot of baggage.

To conservative and fundamentalist Christians, a family must fit the blueprint laid out by their religious authorities, based on what they find in the Bible, or it cannot be a family. But which biblical families are we to emulate? In her article "The Right Is Wrong about Biblical Family Values," my colleague Meg Barnhouse contemplated whether the term "biblical family values" refers to Joseph's brothers selling him into slavery, or to King David sending Bathsheba's husband off to the front to be killed so that he could bed her himself? Or perhaps to King Solomon's family—with his seven hundred wives and three hundred concubines? "I can't see the biblical-family-values people wanting to know about actual biblical families," Barnhouse writes. "I can't see them wanting those families in their neighborhoods or their churches."

In his book *Why Marriage Matters,* Evan Wolfson of the group Freedom to Marry asks us to "imagine that the U.S. Constitution were amended to embody a literal interpretation of what the Bible says about marriage." Here are several options, taken from an e-mail that was widely circulated a couple of years ago and later entered into the Congressional Record by Congressman Jim McDermott of Washington:

- Marriage shall consist of a union between one man and one or more women.
- Marriage shall not impede a man's right to take concubines in addition to his wife or wives.
- If a married man dies, his brother has to marry his widow.

This, obviously, is not what the religious Right has in mind. To conservative Christians, the "traditional" family is headed by a breadwinner husband with a subservient homemaker wife; they marry for the purpose of having and raising children.

If anything, however, this conception of the family is modern, not traditional, since it was invented in the 1950s. Moreover, "white middle- or upper-class family" would be a more accurate descriptor for this idealized family unit. Prior to the middle of the twentieth century, multiple generations of a family tended to live together; labor in agriculturally based societies was shared more equally between men and women and across generations. It was the automobile, the Second World War, and rising urbanization that created the nuclear family while pulling people away from the settled communities in which extended families predominated.

Crucially, the newly fledged nuclear family of the 1950s enjoyed a rising standard of living. There was a postwar economic boom taking place, and our government was providing substantial subsidies for education and home financing. Flourishing businesses rewarded loyal employees with raises and retirement benefits, and people often spent their entire working lives with one employer. Corporations and wealthy individuals paid high taxes, in turn helping to finance the government subsidies. And wages rose enough to make it possible for many men to remain the sole breadwinners in their families.

Things have changed. The booming economy and the public subsidies are gone; companies now downsize and relocate to where labor is cheaper instead of rewarding employee loyalty; conservatives in the White House and Congress are working to dismantle most of the safety net that was put in place over the past forty years to protect the nation's most vulnerable families. Many women who might prefer to stay home to raise their children can no longer afford to do so; and in the wake of the women's movement, many women who *could* afford to stay at home no longer *want* to do so.

Families have changed, too—which is not altogether a bad thing. The 1950s were hardly golden years for families if you were black or gay or female. I am African American. My father was born into a family of relative comfort. He was the son of a successful funeral home owner in Bluefield, West Virginia; he was educated at Harvard and spoke seven languages with some fluency. But he was driving a cab on the streets of Detroit in his early forties when he met my mother. The jobs for which his training had prepared him were simply not available to persons of color at that time.

My father died when I was young, and I grew up in Cincinnati. My mother, who had little formal education, could not stay at home; she took whatever work she could find, as a shop clerk and even selling encyclopedias door-to-door. Ozzie and Harriet's family and Donna Reed's family may have been white and middle class, but poor white women and women of color worked throughout the 1950s.

And marriage in the 1950s could be a nightmare—even for the well-off—although no one talked publicly about abuse or alcoholism or incest. If you were a woman in an abusive marriage, you could not borrow money or even take out a credit card in your own name, so leaving a bad marriage was next to impossible.

So the conservatives' one-size-fits-all notion of the "traditional" family is actually a modern invention—and a far from perfect invention at that. It would not have existed at all apart from a set of extraordinary socioeconomic factors. Considered historically, diversity in family patterns has been the rule, not the exception.

But to conservatives and fundamentalists, family diversity sounds the death knell of "the family." James Dobson, founder of Focus on the Family, warned just before same-sex marriage became legal in Massachusetts in 2004: "Barring a miracle, the family as it has been known for more than five millennia will crumble, presaging the fall of Western civilization itself."

Marriage equality—the freedom for any two people to marry according to the dictates of their hearts and regardless of gender—is where political and religious conservatives now direct most of their firepower in the family wars. The Christian Right wants to protect traditional marriage, but like the "traditional" family, marriage as we know it today is a relatively modern phenomenon. Marriage used to be about economics, property, and politics—more about in-laws, according to family historian Stephanie Coontz, than about love. Marriage was considered far too important an economic and political decision to leave to something as irrational as love, although the nineteenth century witnessed a profound change in that regard. By 1965, the U.S. Supreme Court was able, in the case of *Griswold v. Connecticut*, to call marriage "intimate to the degree of being sacred."

The quality of the relationship between two people in a marriage has come to take precedence over marriage's economic and political role. Sociologists point out that this development brought with it its own problems, particularly a sharp rise in divorce rates. People now expect love and happiness in their marriages, and they will more often end them if that happiness evaporates. But if it is an accepted fact that people should be able to marry whom they love, excluding gay and lesbian partners can no longer be justified except by those who believe that gays and lesbians do not deserve the same happiness as everyone else. Such an animus contradicts one of the first principles articulated in this nation's Declaration of Independence—an inalienable right to the pursuit of happiness. The Supreme Court itself, in its 1967 landmark *Loving v. Virginia* decision, which invalidated state bans on interracial marriage, called marriage "one of the 'basic civil rights of man,' fundamental to our very existence and survival."

Of course, marriage is at least as much about shared responsibility as it is about shared rapture. Writer Jonathan Rauch expresses this beautifully in his book *Gay Marriage*: "If I had to pare marriage to its essential core, I would say marriage is two people's lifelong commitment, recognized by law and by society, to care for each other. To get married is to put yourself in another person's hands, and to promise to take that person into your hands, and to do so within a community which expects both of you to keep your word." The gay and lesbian couples who have been fighting for the right to get married have been fighting for the right to participate in that kind of shared responsibility—to be able to care for the person they love. Many of us are all too familiar with instances in which that right has been denied in appallingly unjust and inhumane ways.

High on the list of most married couples' responsibilities is caring for children. Conservatives insist that only "traditional" families should do this, repeating as a mantra that children should be raised by a mother and a father. Several states now have laws banning homosexuals from adopting children, and a new bill was recently proposed in Texas that would not only have made it illegal for a gay couple to adopt or take in a foster child but would actually have *removed* children from stable gay and lesbian families.

In fact there is a fair amount of evidence suggesting that while children may do better in families with two parents—largely because two adults have more financial and emotional resources to offer each other and their children, not because single parents are necessarily bad for children—the sex of the parents matters little. There is also some evidence suggesting that the children of single parents and gay and lesbian families may enjoy some *advantages* over those raised in more traditional families, as they are exposed to the modeling of more options than the traditional gender roles of mom as nurturer and dad as disciplinarian.

The American Academy of Pediatrics weighed in on this issue in 2002 in the journal *Pediatrics*, recognizing that a

> considerable body of professional literature provides evidence that children with parents who are homosexual can have the same advantages and the same expectations for health, adjustment, and development as can children whose parents are heterosexual. When two adults participate in parenting a child, they and the child deserve the serenity that comes with legal recognition.

What counts, the experts agree, is the quality of the parenting and the relationship between the child and the parents.

There is also evidence that happy parents—whether single or married, straight or gay—raise happy children; and that being happily partnered helps adults stay healthier and live longer than those who are single or living with someone with whom they are miserable. Conversely, the experience of discrimination is "toxic to mental health," according to members of the American Psychiatric Association. At their May 2005 convention they endorsed same-sex marriage on the grounds that "same-sex couples experience several kinds of state-sanctioned discrimination that can adversely affect the stability of their relationships and mental health."

"Happiness," E. J. Graff observes, "or even the simple security of being near someone who cares about you, of being responsible not just to yourself but to and for another—is good for you." She concludes that without family—without others we are responsible to and for—"we scarcely seem human." This view seems to resonate with most Americans: Three-quarters of people polled by *Newsweek* in 1990 defined "family" as "a group of people who love and care for each other."

The Right is correct about the importance of the family: families are, after all, where we raise and socialize the next generation of citizens. But families have changed across the millennia—and they remain vastly different across cultures today. Generations of children raised in every type of family setting have grown up to become productive citizens. Thus it appears rather less than imperative that everyone squeeze their families into any one family mold. And whether the religious Right likes it or not, same-sex families are here to stay: a third of female and more than a fifth of male same-sex families today include children under the age of eighteen.

At the end of 2004, Defense Secretary Donald Rumsfeld responded to a soldier's query about why U.S. troops stationed in Iraq were being asked to face down an increasingly violent insurgency without sufficient armor. "You go to war with the army you have," was Rumsfeld's pithy reply.

I propose that the administration and all of its religious Right allies who worry about nontraditional families take Rumsfeld's maxim to heart and accept that we are bravely and quite successfully raising the next generation with the families we have. The "traditional" family enjoyed a very short run to very mixed reviews. Nostalgia for something so historically anomalous is inevitably a dangerous emotion.

Families continue to improvise as they struggle to adapt to the new economic and social realities of the twenty-first century, in part because the United States provides less support for our most vulnerable families than any other affluent nation in the world. What today is called a family crisis is really a *social* crisis, and demonizing families who do not live up to someone else's moralistic values does little to help. As she writes in *In the Name of the Family,* sociologist Judith Stacey believes that "the politics of gender, sexuality, reproduction, and family here are the most politicized, militant and socially divisive in the world, precisely because social structural responses to the decline of the modern family system have been so weak."

So where is the family headed? We are not yet where we are going, wherever that is. But this much is clear: we could learn much from families of color and from gay and lesbian families in this country. Judith Stacey observes that African American women and poor white women have always had to improvise family arrangements because of the necessity of working. Gay families, often shunned by their families of origin, have also had to invent new family forms. As lesbian activist and author Urvashi Vaid wrote (in the foreword to *Hospital Time* by Amy Hoffman): "For gay people, our friends form our nuclear families while our communities take on the role of an extended family system." During the height of the AIDS epidemic especially, these "alternative family structures proved themselves to be as solid and formidable as traditional families are for heterosexual people."

There is no one perfect family form, but different families have strengths that others can learn from. "*All* families are at risk when they're left to face new challenges on their own," Stephanie Coontz reminds us in *The Way We Really Are*. "All families have the potential to rise above their weaknesses when they get support and encouragement from others."

I believe the questions of what a marriage is and what constitutes a family will resolve themselves as people get used to a changed environment. And I am optimistic about the eventual success of the struggle for marriage equality for same-sex couples. Legal structures are catching up with evolving realities: there is a growing body of court decisions that treat long-term same-sex relationships as no different from any other marriage. Public opinion is shifting, too. Polls suggest that younger Americans—our country's future—overwhelmingly support marriage equality for same-sex couples. It was not that long ago that opponents of interracial marriage predicted catastrophe when bans on such marriages were lifted. But the sun did not stop in its tracks, and public opinion came around. In 1968, a year after *Loving v. Virginia*, a Gallup poll found that more than 75 percent of people still disapproved of marriage across racial lines. Today, more than 75 percent tell pollsters that they approve.

The more people become aware that they know more gay people than they realized and also that many gay people are *already* in families—already married and raising children—the more people who formerly feared same-sex marriage will come to understand that a gay or lesbian family poses no threat to anyone else's commitments. Prejudice does not evaporate overnight, but I am optimistic.

Jonathan Rauch would like to see same-sex marriage become a reality state by state—preferably through legislative rather than judicial action. Why? Because then everyone will see that

> [t]he sky will not fall. Civilization will not tumble into the sea. The divorce and illegitimacy rates will not double. They will not even change noticeably. Other states will notice this. They will see married gay couples woven into the fabric of their communities.... Slowly at first and then with increasing enthusiasm, more states will embrace gay marriage—not because they have to, but because it works.

This country's growing pluralism is a blessing—one that the founders of this country could never have imagined but for which they prepared fertile ground by writing their egalitarian ideals into our foundational documents. What we should be doing in this country is continuing to expand the circle of those we include in the promises made in our Constitution. And I believe that despite the backlash we see every time the circle is widened, it never really shrinks back to where it was before. People learn how much less there is to fear than they had feared.

"The arc of the universe is long," said Martin Luther King, quoting nineteenth-century abolitionist preacher Theodore Parker, "but it bends toward justice." This insight is not mere dreaming; it describes our actual history as well as the history we have yet to create.

Strangers No More

HEIDI NEUMARK

I was a stranger and you welcomed me.

—*Matthew* 25:35

After nearly twenty years as a pastor in the South Bronx, I moved to a new congregation, Trinity Lutheran Church in Manhattan. The church sits in the middle of thousands of housing units, with a large public-housing project on one side of the street and pricey condos and co-ops on the other. The two sides are divided by West 100th Street—and so much more. Those on the southern half of the street enjoy doormen, pleasant lobbies, balcony terraces, and clean elevators that work. The northern side has none of these perks, and residents suffer high levels of asthma, probably because the ventilation systems have not been cleaned since the projects were built in the early fifties. There is another group, too, undocumented immigrants, in particular large numbers of Mexicans, who live in scattered apartment buildings, crowded into cubicles off corridors where up to sixty people may share a bathroom. Families with two, three, or more children squeeze into single rooms with no kitchen or closet. Others live in basements where the landlord has carved out an extra rental bonus, basements with only one exit—up narrow, steep flights of stairs meant for boiler maintenance, not for families carrying small children or lugging groceries, laundry, and strollers.

For the most part, people frequent different grocery stores, their children attend different schools, and the residents receive different levels of medical care. Those who order from takeout menus and those who take orders and wash dishes in the kitchen live as neighbors, but remain strangers. Of course, class divisions exist in countless communities. It is only the proximity of the facing buildings on 100th Street that makes the invisible wall so striking—that, and the war on terror, that schools us in fear of strangers (xenophobia) rather than the biblical virtue of hospitality, *(philoxenos)*: literally loving *(philo)* the stranger *(xenos)* as a brother or sister.

Trinity was founded over one hundred years ago as a haven for German immigrants recently come to New York. Now, as the church welcomes migrants from south of the border, we hear new histories. Gabriela was glad when the woman whose groceries she was packing asked if she would come for a day of housework. It was heavy-duty cleaning—washing floors, walls, and windows all day—but Gabriela only thought of being able to buy the new clothes and shoes her children needed. When ten hours had passed and it was time to collect her wages, Gabriela was handed a $10 bill, told that a stinking Mexican who should not be here anyway ought to be grateful, and shown the door.

Gabriela comes to a table in the parish hall where other immigrant women are gathered on a Friday afternoon. She pours out her pain as the others listen, understand, encourage. Victorina is there. She recently took a job at a café—forty-five hours a week for $70, less than $2 an hour with $400 in rent due each month for a tiny room in someone else's apartment. Victorina prays that she doesn't get sick. At the same table, she'd listened to Maria talk about her medical ordeal. Maria traveled here from El Salvador during the civil war back in 1987. She would have qualified for legal papers at one point, but no one ever explained that to her.

When I visited Maria to find out the results of a medical test shortly after the last presidential election, I found her sobbing in front of the TV, watching the news from Iraq. "Don't they realize that nothing good can come from this war? War killed my father, my sister, my eleven-year-old brother." Maria pushed her pants leg up to show her deeply scarred leg, struck by shrapnel. She told of hiding under her bed for two weeks. It was the war that led her across the border to find safety. "No soy terrorista! " she sobbed. "I am not a terrorist! Why do they think I'm a terrorist? All I do is take my children to school, clean houses, cook, pick my children up, cook, and spend the evening with them."

When she stopped crying, I asked about the tests. She was scheduled for a sonogram after months of chest pain and numerous emergency-room visits. Doctors had been mystified by her hard, swollen belly, which made her appear eight months' pregnant. Maria rubbed her stomach, which alternately burned and ached, and told me, "I couldn't get the tests done. I had to pay in cash and I don't have that much money." The hospital had demanded $1,000 in cash to do the sonogram. One medication seemed to help, but once the free sample was gone, Maria had to pay about $10 a pill. Church members chipped in to buy a two-month supply. This was the beginning of many frustrated attempts to take Jesus's words to heart: "When was it that we saw you sick and did not care for you?" We kept bumping up against an unworkable system that no single congregation could repair.

A seminary student working at Trinity spent hours listening to Maria and preparing an English transcript of her medical history to clarify things for the next clinic visit, given that every visit meant a different doctor and no guarantee of anyone who could understand Spanish. Then, as if by miraculous intervention, two doctors came to the church office with flyers to announce that they wanted to see more patients at the clinic right next door. I sped to Maria's apartment with the good news. She went the next morning, right after taking her daughters to school: her stomach was larger (she was told that "it" had transmuted from a grapefruit to a soccer ball) and her heart weaker. When she returned in the afternoon, I could see that any medical wonders being dispensed at the clinic had passed by Maria. She had spent the day standing in line for hours, no chairs or water in sight, just to be told that only those who were HIV positive or addicted to drugs could be seen. The next morning, I went over to find out what was going on. I, too, was confronted by guards who instructed me to get in the long line and wait my turn. "But I want to see one of these doctors," I said, waving one of the flyers, which now seemed to have all the gravitas of a carnival broadside promoting never-before-seen marvels and wonders: "Come one and all! Come see real doctors! Come see doctors who want to see more patients!!!" As far as the guards on clinic duty were concerned, my flyer was a sham. Finally, I found a believer—the building manager, whose closed office Maria would have never dared to enter. The doctors were only a short walk down the corridor, but the guards had no clue, even though they worked in the same clinic for the same city health department.

Shortly after this episode, we found an insurance that Maria qualified for and could manage to pay. She went to an emergency room with her new insurance card and was scheduled for an operation the next day. Her mystery ailment was a mystery no more: sick while undocumented and uninsured (a condition that is sometimes fatal). A huge tumor was removed and the pressure on her heart subsided. The stress on her four daughters let up, too, and for the first time in months, the oldest, Trini, age eleven, was able to fall asleep without crying. Those who worry that too much money is going into extensive medical care for the undocumented may be relieved to know that this is not always true.

Maria, Victorina, and Gabriela were strangers to one another, shy at first, uncertain, but they have become sisters at the table, *hermanas*. They listen, encourage, hug, pray, cook, and sometimes dance together. They share tips of where to find work with decent people. Together, at the table, they belong. They are part of this parish family. In Spanish, the word for parish is *parroquia*, even closer than the English as a derivative from the Greek *paroikia*. Paroikia, as the Bible makes clear, indicates a place of exile, a place where you might find one who is a *paroikos*, a stranger, one who sojourns in a foreign land or is a resident alien. It is instructive that our parishes are intended to be places of hospitality for the paroikos. Such ministry is not a sideline but our core identity as a church, an identity with a long history.

Abraham and Sarah were immigrants who left the land of their birth to sojourn toward a future where they would become resident aliens. Joseph was caught up in whirlwind of familial, economic, and international conflicts as a detained alien whose traumatic journey ultimately gained him legal status and enabled him to feed his family back home. Moses, a child truly left behind, became a resident alien in Midian and the divinely appointed *coyote* who led a band of desperate refugees on a desert trek toward freedom. The Israelites later spent many years living in exile, resident aliens. Ruth remained with Naomi as a paroikos in Israel, a migrant eager for subsistence fieldwork, grateful for the gleanings left on the ground by those who owned the land. Thus Ruth, the Moabite, joined Bathsheba, the Hittite, and Tamar and Rahab, both Canaanites, as aliens on the family tree of Jesus according to St. Matthew's genealogy. If the word *alien* is disconcerting and conjures up images of oddballs from outer space, it is just as disorienting to people like my husband, who came from Argentina on Pam Am (rather than a spaceship) and saw his face on the green card staring back above the label: "resident alien."

We don't label our biblical ancestors as suspect strangers or terrorists; we honor them and love them as foremothers and forefathers of our faith. We regularly welcome them into our churches and homes. We hail their stories as holy and introduce them to our children and our grandchildren. But what if they appeared today? What would happen to Moses and his band at the Arizona border? Would Joseph have remained in detention until he was deported to perish with his family in the famine? Would we deny health care to Sarah and leave Ruth to try and survive off scraps discarded by people like the woman who handed $10 to Gabriela?

When the Hebrew people finally crossed the border they were told: "You shall not oppress a resident alien; you know the heart of an alien, for you were aliens in the land of Egypt" (Exodus 23:9). As Christians, we have an even stronger mandate. "He was in the world and the world came into being through him, yet the world did not know him" (John 1:10) Jesus came among us as a stranger and quickly became a political refugee when Mary and Joseph fled to Egypt, hoping to escape a brutal military regime, like many who come here seeking asylum. When the two disciples on the road to Emmaus call Jesus a stranger, a paroikos, it is a word that had long been part of God's walk with humanity: Jesus as resident alien, Jesus as one whose life was given over to border crossings and radical hospitality.

Jesus lived in a society ordered by clear demarcations, sorting and separating people by an elaborate system of purity codes that stood as firmly as the Separation Wall being built in the Holy Land today, as impenetrable as many would like our borders to become. The codes created no-trespassing zones of untouchability that had particular impact on the chronically ill, disfigured, or handicapped, on women, on foreigners and those of different ethnic groups and origins. Additionally, anyone of unorthodox or questionable lifestyle remained on the wrong side of the border. In contrast, Jesus frequently lifted up the faith and witness of foreigners who had no legal standing, often Samaritans who were so despised that Samaritan girls were said to menstruate from the cradle, a triple taboo involving foreigners, women, and blood. And yet, it was from a Samaritan woman that Jesus sought a drink when he was thirsty in the desert and it was to a Samaritan woman that Jesus opened a well of wisdom and new life.

It is profoundly ironic that some contemporary followers of Jesus use religious tradition as a reason to resist the vision of God doing a new thing in these days, whether that be the acceptance of partnered gay clergy in some denominations or the ordination of women in others. Jesus consistently broke with many centuries-old traditions in the name of a higher law.

A large photo on the front page of the *New York Times* shows a group of clergy taking a strong ecumenical stand, the only such show of solidarity to make the front page in what seems like years. It was a highly public witness of Christians, Jews, and Muslims joined in a city racked by hatred and division—Jerusalem. And what was it that at last brought the people of faith together? Abdel Aziz Bukhari, a Sufi sheik, explained: "We can't permit anybody to come and make the Holy City dirty. This is very ugly and very nasty to have these people come to Jerusalem." Who are they who would pollute the unstained streets of Jerusalem? They were participants in a gay pride festival. "This is not the homo land, this is the Holy Land," one of the leaders said at their news conference, calling the festival "the spiritual rape of the Holy City." It is disheartening to see that what brings the faiths together is hatred and fear and that this is the way religion is frequently portrayed in the public square. It's hard to understand how Jesus fits into this picture when the gospels portray him as flouting tradition to welcome, touch, heal, and dine with those considered "very ugly and very nasty" in their day.

The early church continued to struggle to live out these values of hospitality. Peter himself wrestled with the call to depart from venerable spiritual tradition when his missionary journey took him into Gentile territory. When Peter is up on the roof praying, he sees a tablecloth filled with forbidden foods drop into his lap and he hears God telling him to dig in. Peter is horrified. He must be hearing wrong, because this is just plain ugly and nasty—"By no means Lord; for I have never eaten anything that is profane or unclean!" But Peter's eyes are eventually opened and he finds himself eating with his Gentile sisters and brothers, their hair still damp from baptism.

In a recent excavation around the Jerusalem temple, a broken pillar was found with these words inscribed on it: "No man of another race is to enter within the fence and enclosure around the Temple. Whoever is caught will have only himself to thank for the death which follows." Imagine the shift in thought and emotion required for Peter to accept the hospitality of a Gentile household and for Paul to write these words:

> Now in Christ Jesus you who once were far off [the Gentiles] have been brought near by the blood of Christ. For he is our peace; in his flesh he has made both groups into one and has broken down the dividing wall, that is, the hostility between us. He has abolished the law with its commandments and ordinances, that he might create in himself one new humanity in place of the two, thus making peace, and might reconcile both groups to God in one body through the cross. . . . So then you are no longer strangers and aliens, but you are citizens with the saints and also members of the household of God. (Ephesians 2:13–16,19)

Paul is saying what Jesus taught: the borders are open, let the uncircumcised come in as full citizens in our household of faith. It's equivalent to telling a company of border guards that now they will be sharing tortillas with the very undocumented people they were trained to view as terrorist suspects. Precisely! So why is it that a number of Arizona megachurches scour their neighborhoods and canvas "everyone," intentionally ignoring the many Mexican immigrants in their midst? One such church raises a large American flag, but no cross. "We've tried to bring down those visual cues that scare people off," the pastor said. The Roman Empire knew that feeling.

The household hospitality practiced by Christians was in direct opposition to the hierarchical structure of the Roman Empire. Cicero is instructive. He describes the ruling elite's view of professions as divided among the worthy, the unworthy, and the downright sordid, *sordidum*. While those who worked with their hands were not on the level of beggars, they were never able to reach the upper classes or to become social insiders. For instance, while purple fabric was desirable, the work of creating it was a sordidum job done by sordidum people who lived apart. Today, many immigrants are welcome to sew clothing or build gadgets at *maquilas* across the border, but they shouldn't expect anyone to stop the machines just because hundreds of their sordidum coworkers are raped and murdered. They are even welcome to do the sordidum jobs on this side, picking fruits and vegetables, washing dishes, cleaning homes, caring for children, but their sordidum children cannot get papers so they cannot qualify for financial aid to attend college.

Breaking this pattern to live toward the hospitality that genuinely loves strangers as brothers and sisters requires that we are able to communicate with one another. This demands careful intentionality, especially among those who don't speak each other's language. "It's too early in the morning for Spanish," complained one member after our first bilingual service. Some probably felt that it was too early for English, too, but almost everyone decided that they wanted to worship together on a regular basis, which turns out to be about nine times a year. Other

Sundays, we worship separately in English or in Spanish. We are together enough so that what was once an alien tradition is becoming our tradition. Now no one even wants to imagine Palm Sunday without an outdoor procession led by a mariachi band in full regalia as neighbors lean out of windows to see and smile and clap. A Mexican father photographs his son singing a gospel song with the children's choir. An African American mother comments approvingly on the pride she sees in six- and seven-year-old immigrant children in peacock feather headdresses doing an Aztec dance down the aisle, stamping out rhythms that ring from ankle bracelets covered in bottle caps (when the teacher could not find the traditional shells used in Mexico, he improvised with Corona caps). What did we do in mid-December without a fragrant sanctuary set abloom with dozens and dozens of roses as part of the Guadalupe celebration, while aromas of tamales and simmering cinnamon rice fill the downstairs hall?

The guests have now become the hosts; those who were strangers have spent all day in the kitchen to prepare a feast of hospitality for the entire congregation. In many churches, kitchen rights are an important sign of belonging. The right to use the stove or go into the refrigerator is a closely guarded privilege. Only those inducted into the kitchen mysteries know where to find a certain size dish or cutting board. Sometimes keys are needed. And so the friendly kitchen takeover by newcomers was an important milestone at the church. It probably helped that everyone knew good food was on the way. Few people in New York have trouble enjoying one another's cuisines. Fried chicken with all the soul food sides, *ingera* bread dipped in spicy stew from Eritrea, *pasteles* from Puerto Rico, Italian pasta, Mexican chicken with mole sauce, and unsold Starbucks pastries, thanks to an underpaid dancer who works the Saturday night shift—no one turns away from such potluck feasts where the only downside is the calories. But sharing food and table fellowship, upstairs and down, is not enough.

Santo, Santo, Santo, we sing around the table set with bread and wine: Holy, Holy, Holy. When that song was first sung around the throne of

God, as recorded in the book of Revelation, the choir was raising its voice to honor a holy power in resistance and opposition to the powers of Rome that maintained control by keeping everyone in his or her place. This was Roman peace, the Pax Romana. The multicultural songs of praise that rang in John's ears during his state-imposed exile were radically different: "I looked and there was a great multitude... from every nation, from all tribes and peoples and languages standing before the throne and before the Lamb... these are they who have come out of the great ordeal," John is told (Revelation 7:9, 14). The great ordeal was pretty much the opposite of the great New Deal. John was lucky that his fate was only forced seclusion on the isle of Patmos at a time when allegiance to the emperor's religious preference was equated with political loyalty, and the repercussions for those who refused to comply were taking an increasingly nasty turn. John's isolation on Patmos was shared by many who had lived in the center of the world's superpower but found themselves pushed to the edge as a permanent underclass.

For those who sing praises to the One on Revelation's throne, what happens at the tables of worship and fellowship overturns the tables of power as well. And so at our last congregational meeting, the church voted that the council must be bilingual and must include members whose primary language is Spanish. This means reports must be in earlier for translation. It means a changed agenda, more seats at the table where decisions are made, more voices heard, different issues to consider: "So then you are no longer strangers and aliens, but you are citizens with the saints and also members of the household of God." This household is as countercultural today as it was when John was banished to Patmos. It is antithetical to the Pax desired in numbers of churches—and yet, it is where we meet Jesus.

In Luke's Resurrection account, when Jesus appears on the road to Emmaus, it is as a stranger. "Are you the only stranger in Jerusalem who does not know the things that have taken place there in these days?" asks one of the wayfarers whom Jesus meets incognito. "We had hoped that he [Jesus of Nazareth] was the one to redeem us," they continue. Then the grieving disciples open their doors in hospitality to this resident alien who transforms before their eyes from guest to host: "When he was at table with them, he took bread, blessed and broke it, and gave it to them. Then their eyes were opened and they recognized him" (Luke 24:30–31).

Our own Emmaus Sunday took place two weeks after Easter. Most of our growing number of Spanish-speaking members cannot yet converse in English, and an even larger number of others know next to nada in Spanish. This makes communication beyond nods and smiles difficult. So for our Emmaus Sunday, we lined up a cadre of bilingual members to serve as translators and assigned each one to a pair on opposite sides of the language border. For about an hour, they chatted away, finding surprising points of commonality and striking places of difference, newly present to one another as sisters and brothers, having their eyes opened to Jesus walking among us, beside us, within us.

We had hoped, the saddened disciples said. For them, hope was in the past tense. I confess that sometimes when I see the divisions that mark our city and nation and world and find them mirrored in our churches, I, too, lose the spring in my step. Two men sipping coffee in a parish hall give me hope. One of them is tall, blond, and pale. The other is short with black hair and skin bronzed by sun seeping through his genes for centuries. One man just got his master's degree in social work. The other never went beyond the fourth grade. One speaks only English, the other Spanish. When they needed a place to live in New York City, one went to his computer and searched on Craig's List, eventually finding a small apartment that would appear palatial compared with the tiny room the other man found by word of mouth for himself, his pregnant wife, and daughter. One has a new job doing what he has always wanted to do, working with drug addicts seeking recovery. The other works a double shift washing dishes.

Their names are Brian and Javier. It would seem that they share little apart from their mutual enjoyment of coffee. But last December, they found themselves traveling the same road. In Javier's case it was a journey back to Mexico: his brother died suddenly in New York, undocumented and afraid to seek medical help until it was too late. Nothing seemed more important to Javier than accompanying his sister-in-law to take his brother's body back to Mexico for burial. The journey meant leaving his pregnant wife, daughter, and newly fatherless niece and nephew. It also meant having to cross the border back without papers, chancing deportation, detention, or death. It was a high-risk journey, which could cut him off from his family forever. Javier came to church and shared his anxiety as well as his conviction of the trip's necessity. We sat together and prayed.

The same week that Javier was setting out for Mexico, Brian was leaving for Iowa, flying home to tell his family over Christmas that he is gay. Brian is a young man who would make many parents proud. While studying for his master's, he worked for the Red Cross, attending to families in crisis after fires, suicides, and other catastrophes. He faithfully attends church where he serves on the council and is a leader for congregational community organizing work and the new young adult ministry. But despite his recent degree and new job, Brian didn't have high expectations of any congratulatory celebrations in his honor over the holiday. He had endured numerous conversations in his religiously conservative family about "homos going to hell." Still, it was so achingly clear in listening to him talk that he yearned for a Christmas miracle. Like Javier, he was embarking on a high-risk journey that could cut him off from his family forever. He came to church and shared his anxiety as well as his conviction of the trip's necessity. We sat together and prayed.

We knew stories of similar journeys taken by others in the GLBT community and by immigrants that proved to be disastrous. Tragic news of groups who die of dehydration comes every year beginning in April, when Sonoran Desert temperatures daily climb to three digits. Often the trip takes longer than people anticipate and it is easy to get lost. The *coyotes*, whom many migrants pay to guide them, might leave markers such as a sneaker tied to a bush or a ribbon on a cactus, but sometimes these fragile signposts disappear; this leaves people stranded, uncertain of which way to go. The decent *coyotes* may also leave jugs of water buried at key places, but not all are trustworthy. Some simply rob the migrants of money and valuables and abandon them.

There are groups like Humane Borders, Fronteras Compasivos, that tend water stations, marked by tall blue flags that rise higher than the tallest saguaro cactus, blue flags easily visible for miles across the flat expanses of the desert. The water stations have saved many lives, but the numbers of those driven into the desert by desperation are increasing, too, and many continue to die, struck down by scorching heat.

Javier remembers his last trip, climbing through the barbed wire fence; he said he didn't even feel it cutting at the time. The scars came later, and other barbs. Javier doesn't need to know English to read the tears in many eyes.

Brian's seen and heard it, too—the looks, the comments—ever since he was a teenager. He has his own share of scars. Studies show that half of all homeless youth are lesbian or gay, many kicked out by intolerant families. Their numbers are growing, ironically, due to a shift in popular culture with mainstream programs like *Queer Eye for the Straight Guy*, *Will and Grace*, and the Emmy-winning talk show hosted by Ellen DeGeneres. The acceptance implied in these programs has motivated young people to come out to families who continue to dwell on a different side of the cultural divide. Carl Siciliano, the director of Manhattan's largest shelter for gay youth, anguishes about teens unable to find a safe place of welcome. Too many end up trying to fend for themselves on streets that offer little besides drugs, hustling, and the HIV virus. One oasis in this urban desert, the Ali Forney Center, has twelve beds for GLBT youth. The waiting list for a bed in that shelter has close to one hundred names on it, and a troubling percentage of these youth will end up dead by their own hand. They, too, are perishing in the desert, struck down by the scorching heat of judgment in a spiritual landscape where countless steeples that might rise up like blue flags of hope have become a different kind of marker, signaling condemnation.

For immigrants, there is a way to skirt death in the desert. It's called *cruzando por liñas*. This involves passing as a different person, using the legal documents belonging to someone with a similar face. It can make for a much smoother passage across the border, because you can go directly, without the long, dangerous route through the desert, but it's getting tougher. The guards are more thorough, with their competence under question by the self-appointed civilian militia. *Cruzando por liñas* comes at a high price, $2,500 a person or more, and the anxiety is high, too, the fear of being discovered for who one truly is, or is not. In any case, Javier and his sister-in-law could not pay the price for false documents, so they would have to risk the journey, vulnerable to the elements and dependent on the goodness of their *coyote*.

Brian also found it too costly to pass as someone else. He no longer had the desire or wherewithal to offer a false face to his family. He, too, would have to risk the journey, vulnerable and hoping for the goodness of others.

Brian and Javier's journeys ended in the same place, the sanctuary of the church, giving thanks to God. Brian got his Christmas miracle. Against all expectation, his family, including his father, about whom he was most concerned, embraced him with acceptance. Javier and his sister-in-law arrived back as well, months later, but before the baby was born.

"I am thirsty," he said, no stranger to our predicament, his throat dry and parched as the Arizona desert. The crown of thorns sharp as barbed wire. *I am thirsty*. Thirsty on the *frontera* of life and death. Thirsty in the cries of our sisters and brothers, and of all the children left behind. *One of the soldiers pierced his side with a spear and at once blood and water came out.*

A steeple rises over West 100th Street like a blue flag in the desert to say: Here is water, here is welcome, here is life. A year ago, a slate tile fell off that steeple and narrowly missed hitting someone walking by. Now a protective sidewalk bridge has been put up as we struggle to raise money for expensive repairs. There is a lot of work to do—on that steeple, and so many others.

After communion, we go downstairs for coffee. Brian is there, and Javier—strangers no more.

The iPod, the Cell Phone, and the Church: Discipleship, Consumer Culture, and a Globalized World

VINCENT MILLER

They are like trees planted by streams of water.

—*Psalm 1:3*

Consumerism. Most likely if you are reading this book you are generally opposed to it. Critiquing it from a religious perspective is like shooting fish in a barrel. We all more or less recognize the problems, we all know the elements of our religious traditions that consumerism conflicts with, and yet we all manage to live lives that are largely indistinguishable from those of neighbors who lack these convictions. Sociologist Robert Bocock reports that the United States is both the world leader in consumption and by far the most religious of the developed capitalist nations. Indeed, the background religious tradition in America—Puritanism—is deeply suspicious of consumption and worldly indulgence.[1] Clearly, we are involved in a deep-level disconnect around consumerism.

This disconnect could simply be labeled moral weakness or hypocrisy in the face of consumerism's impressive temptations. But this is not the only disconnect we experience in our lives. We are tugged and pulled by a thousand impulses and desires: spiritual paths we desire to follow, communities we desire to build, political actions we desire to take. Yet we find it terribly difficult to put these great desires into action.

Perhaps there is some underlying kinship among all of these disconnects. Consumerism poses more than another case of hypocrisy. Consumerism draws together and intensifies elements of the common culture that actively *feed* a disconnect between faith and practice. Consumerism and its cultural cousin, globalization, are profound cultural dynamics that are changing the way that we relate to our religious traditions and attempt to put them into practice.

We are all used to talking about consumerism in terms of selfish materialism. Globalization is frequently equated with free-market ideology, which drives our current economic age. There is truth in these representations. But it is their deeper cultural impacts that pose the most profound challenge.

Both consumer culture and globalization are powerful engines for cultural fragmentation. Consumer culture takes traditions apart, reducing them to collections of disconnected symbols, beliefs, and practices. Globalization frees us from the confines of space and in the process takes communities apart. It opens traditional, social, and religious spaces up to the freedom of choice. In many cases, this is clearly a good thing, but it has a downside as well. It renders our ability to carry out meaningful social and political actions increasingly dependent on our individual ability to sustain them. In response to these dynamics, we must reconsider the value of particular grounded communities and of our traditional religious pathways.

Consumerism shapes consciousness and behavior at levels far deeper than the manifestations we all recognize—the clamoring for new styles of $500 designer jeans, for example. On this deeper level, consumerism remakes our habits and practices, inviting us to treat other persons as well as culture, politics, and religious beliefs as if *these* were also consumables.

The same with globalization: there is both its manifest expressions and its less-recognized effects. We all recognize the global visions and prognostications uttered at the annual Davos Forum as expressions of globalization, but we might not notice how someone running an anti-U.N. Web site out of his basement is using the technologies and practices of globalization as much as the billionaires who fly to Switzerland.

Two widely used personal technologies—the iPod and the cell phone—serve as helpful metaphors for consumer culture and globalization. They illustrate profound changes that are taking place in our cultural and religious practices that are changing our relationship with our beliefs. How do these new practices impinge upon more traditional practices associated with the parish or congregation? This is an important question because the local church is the primary nexus for integrating gospel values and everyday life.

The iPod and Consumer Culture

There are myriad ways in which the iPod symbolizes the workings of consumer culture. It is what marketers call a "transformative product"; it has both created an entirely new market—digital music players—and established itself as an instantly recognizable brand. Two years ago a wave of white earbud headphones crested on campus. Suddenly everyone had them. To use the device is to be part of the brand, to become a walking advertisement, an everyday endorser.

But the iPod is most interesting not as an example of an object of consumption itself but as a device that facilitates a certain *kind* of consumption, not of things but of culture. As a tool for consuming culture it tells us a lot about how consumers are inclined to relate to culture. Consumer culture trains us to relate to culture in a certain way, and this has enormous consequences for how we relate to religious culture as well.

What does the iPod teach us? Consider what it does and how it is used. It enables a new practice of music, one that might be just as significant as earlier technical innovations such as the phonograph and the radio. Both of those brought music consumption to the masses. Instead of having to perform music oneself, or pay others to do it, people were given easy access to a range of music. In the process, music listening was changed. It went from a participatory skill or special event to a background activity that could be integrated into the rhythm of daily life. These changes weren't limited to music. They were cultural as well. They contributed to the passive reception of culture as an object of consumption. Cultures may flourish by handing on the same music from generation to generation, but recording companies certainly do not.

As a result, culture became commercialized, folk traditions were supplanted, and cultural change was accelerated in service of commerce.

The iPod continues these trends and introduces new changes in the way we relate to music and, thus, culture. Key among these is the way the iPod enables the disembedding of songs from their contexts. There is no need to switch CDs or to spend time cueing up the track you want to listen to; it provides easy and random access to all of the songs in your library. Indeed, file-exchange software and legal digital music stores have made it common to buy just the song you want, rather than to waste money on the whole album. Thus, people are more likely to get only the highlights, the singles marketed as hits. So-called "deep album tracks"—those quirky masterpieces that may demand more of listeners—are more likely to go unheard.

This narrowing of exposure through increased convenience exists in tension with a simultaneous greater access to music. It is now much easier then ever to sample a diverse range of music. And the selection is unprecedented. One online digital music store has more than 1 million songs from all the major labels and more than six hundred smaller, independent labels. It offers many albums that are out of print.

The iPod has also fed the decline of shared listening. Whatever one thinks about the banality of Top 40 music, it provided shared cultural touch points, a communally remembered soundtrack of memory. Contrast this with what I witnessed in my neighborhood the other day: a couple out running together, each with the white earbuds and sleek gadgets in hand. Each was probably listening to his or her own personal exercise mix. Jogging together . . . alone. Notice how the technology encourages such individual choice. They could load a shared song list on both and carefully press play simultaneously. But that involves some hassle. Look around, you'll now see cars full of teenagers cruising around, each with his or her own iPod, in a private musical space.

The iPod doesn't just allow personal playlists, it is designed for them. We all have a personal top twenty or so songs. I have always been filled with joy at the serendipity when one of my favorites would come on the radio. I would wait in the parking lot or driveway until the song ended.

The rest of life would have to wait during a rare playing of Traffic's 11:41-minute "Low Spark of High Heeled Boys." Now, on the iPod, they are all on constant queue and can be paused. My bike ride to work is now my personal all-time favorites show. A host of recent newspaper articles note how socially significant playlists have become. Apple's iTunes—the computer software companion to the iPod—allows sharing music over office networks. People evaluate each other based on their choices. When President Bush's playlist was publicized, many noted his choice of John Fogerty's banal "Centerfield" over the same artist's more biting (and personally relevant) anthem, "Fortunate Son." Another recent article discussed the particular trauma people feel when their iPod is stolen. They grieve not the loss of an expensive gadget but the violation that comes when a stranger has their playlist.[2]

Religion: iPod Style

What does this have to do with religion? It correlates quite well with how "spirituality" is currently understood as the preferred form of religious practice; spirituality as distinguished from religion, which is understood to be bound up with tradition and institutions. Spirituality in this sense privileges the individual quest as the fundamental way of encountering the divine. Even those who still practice the religion of their childhood are expected to be able to account for how they chose it themselves.

The expectation of choice presumes that religious traditions are readily accessible. That one can, without much difficulty, evaluate whether Buddhism, Carmelite spirituality, or the Ignatian Exercises are "for you" or not. It also privileges individual syntheses. People are encouraged to take elements from multiple traditions or subtraditions and work them into their own personal spirituality—a form of religious belief very much like the workings of the iPod.

There are problems with this sort of religious life. But I want to distinguish my concerns from the commonly heard critique that consumerist spirituality is intrinsically narcissistic. This view assumes that when left to their own lights, people will chose only the easiest, least challenging, most accommodating options. I would counter that much depends on one's theology of grace. My own Catholic tradition cannot accept so pessimistic an assumption. There is no reason to believe that contemporary believers are any less profound than those of days past.

Indeed, contemporary believers have access to an unprecedented range of profound religious material. The Paulist Classics of Western Spirituality series serves as an example of all that is good about this dynamic. It comprises more than 130 authors and traditions, offered in expert translations with introductions by scholarly experts. This series and countless other books and other media bring the riches of Christian and other religious traditions to the homes of millions of believers. A cultural system that produces a market like that certainly can't be all bad.

But there are problems, nonetheless. They have to do with how we encounter, use, and share religious material. Consumer culture trains us to engage elements of religious traditions as disconnected fragments. They come to us shorn of the interconnections with other symbols and doctrines that together weave a worldview. Commodified pieces of religious traditions are less likely to be complex, to make demands upon us that challenge us to live differently. They are ground down, like shiny, polished stones, more likely to conform to the preexisting shape of our lives rather than to challenge it.

For example, we get the Ten Commandments proposed as a Christian standard of morality but largely reduced to injunctions against adultery, theft, and murder—things that most of us manage to avoid on most days with little problem. Surprisingly little attention is given to the way in which Jesus—in good Jewish fashion—understood the Commandments as much more difficult demands: "Love God with all of your heart, soul and mind," and "Love your neighbor as yourself." The relatively safe morality of conventional interpretations of the Commandments is substituted for the much more complex and difficult demands of Jesus in the Beatitudes.

We also get further reinforcement for the tendency in Christianity to separate God's forgiveness from our ongoing sinfulness. In the famous words of H. Richard Niebuhr about early-twentieth-century liberal theology: "A God without wrath brought men without sin into a kingdom without judgment through the ministrations of a Christ without a Cross." The crucifix or cross becomes a symbol of God's mercy only, and we cease to see it also as sober illustration of the cost of faithfulness to God's Good News. And on the other side, justice is separated from mercy and devolves into a blasphemous legitimation of vengeance. In each case, elements of a religious tradition are treated in abstraction from their broader doctrinal and devotional connections. They are ground down into small pieces that conform to the cultural status quo. Thus we see the current political impasse for Christianity in America. Belief is cleanly divided along partisan lines. The complexities of the Christian tradition seemingly lack sufficient power to challenge the divisions of the political status quo.

A second problem with consumer culture arises from another way that it fragments religious traditions. We encounter and are tempted to use religious material in a manner disconnected from the communities, practices, and institutions that connect them to a concrete form of life. This seriously inhibits our spiritual beliefs and values from having any transformative effect upon our lives. As seekers in the spiritual marketplace (to use Wade Clark Roof's term), we sample a hundred profound truths but our lives remain unchanged. For that we need complex shared beliefs and practices, community support, and challenge.

Consider the difference between quietly, privately turning your heart to God at various times throughout the day and the practice of daily liturgical prayer, like the Christian Prayer of the Hours or the Muslim practice of *Salat,* praying certain prayers with certain gestures five times a day. Notice how the latter two begin to structure a different way of life, while the first conforms to the shape of the world we already live in. Notice as well how the latter do not need to rely on sheer willpower; rather, they provide a rhythm for life to follow.

Or consider the contrast between going to Barnes and Noble, choosing a Bible translation from the shelf, and selecting some passages to reflect upon individually; and hearing the scriptures proclaimed in a worshipping community that carries on a continuing discussion about how to best live it out. In the first instance, the effects all depend on your capacity to interpret the text and your willpower in trying to respond. In the second, you draw from the broader resources of the community in interpreting the text, and you engage with others in working through a faithful response.

In both cases the second examples put belief into a lived context that is more likely to help believers translate their convictions into practice. They show how structures and disciplines can help believers to resist and even transform the status quo.

Consumer culture reinforces an understanding of spirituality as the sum of individual quests for meanings. The meanings discovered by such quests undoubtedly help people cope with the difficulties of everyday life, but they rarely cohere into a worldview that challenges it. Consumer culture shakes religious traditions through a great sieve that reduces their complex pieces and practices to small, easily consumed fragments that, like sand, conform to the shape of the container of everyday life in the modern world.

Christian spirituality in its fullness is more than a personal set of meanings. It is a particular form of life through which believers respond to God's grace in a particular manner, deepening their living of the Christian life in terms of both inward transformation and outward discipleship. Spirituality is not only a matter of experience, symbol, and belief but also of practices, communal structures, institutions, and spaces.

Franciscan spirituality provides a clear example. It combines a profoundly affective spirituality that embraces emotion, desire, and the love of nature with very concrete practices and places—vows of poverty and mendicancy, solidarity with the poor and outcasts, withdrawal to the countryside. St. Francis's romantic engagement with the crucified Christ developed through engagement with lepers and the poor and drew him out of the comforts of Assisi to its margins in society and nature. You can talk about either aspect in abstraction from the other—

mystical love of Christ or solidarity with the poor. But only *together* do they constitute the fullness of Franciscan spirituality. The threat of consumer culture is not that it deprives us of such grand spiritual visions but that it trains us to engage them in a manner that severs their necessary connections with those particular spaces and practices that lend them their great transformative power.

The Cell Phone and Globalization

Standing as a metaphor for the rapid communications technologies of globalization, the cell phone illuminates profound changes in both how we imagine and practice space. Note how people begin their calls: "Hi, it's me. I'm just getting off the plane . . . ," "I'm at the store . . . ," "I'm waiting in the checkout line . . . ," and so on. That second phrase has become essential. I call this "placing." We now need to "place" ourselves when we use the phone. Landlines locate us in a particular place, but wireless networks follow us anywhere. We know whom we are talking to, but we no longer know where they are. There is, in this practice of placing, a profound change in our relationship to space. We may tell the person we are talking to where we are, but in some ways the very act of calling takes us out of that space. We invoke physical place even as we leave it. Social space becomes detached from physical location. We aren't being *with* the people at the baggage claim; we're being *with* someone miles away on the phone. The network becomes a new space—one that provides an option to be anywhere we choose.

How fast things have changed! Influential accounts of the cultural effects of globalization written just a few years ago didn't notice this change wrought by the cell phone. They still spoke of how the global comes "into" our domestic space, in the form of phone calls or mass media. In that short period of time, we have shifted to the new social space of networks. Communication comes to our cell phones or e-mail or IM accounts. What used to be called private or domestic space is now very possibly wherever we are logged in to the network. Having just adjusted to not assuming people talking to themselves while they walk down the sidewalk are mentally ill, we now have to adjust to the new construction of domestic space—people having intimate conversations on cell phones in public. In the past month, I've twice witnessed a student walking across campus engaged in an emotional phone conversation, not just teary eyed but sobbing.

There is a lot that is good about this. Cell phones help us maintain relationships in a migratory society. Two generations ago, my great-uncle left Pittsburgh for Chicago and was never heard from again. Things are very different today. My brother and I live in cities eight hundred miles apart, and his job requires a lot of travel. But I call his cell phone and talk to him anywhere. My students report not just knowing people all over the world, but maintaining frequent contact with friends who have gone abroad or whom they met when they were abroad themselves. This new accessibility offers much to religion and discipleship that we must consider.

But there are also downsides to this change in our relationship with space. Consider how the cell phone insulates us from the frictions of happenstance—those unforeseen and unplanned events that bring us fortune and woe, joys and challenges. Stuck waiting for a bus? There's no need to make small talk with strangers; call your friends. You can reach them even if they are stuck at a different bus stop themselves. But with this convenience comes the loss of the chance meeting that results in an unexpected friend or a lifetime love affair. We also lose the sacrificial conversation with the lonely and the uncomfortable request from the needy. The past decade has witnessed a decline of roadside Good Samaritanism. Everyone now presumably has cell phones and can call for his or her own help from professionals and friends.

It would be easy to construe this in moral terms. But my point is not that cell phones make us bad people who don't care about what is going on around us, who blithely leave widows and orphans stranded on the sides of roads to change their own tires. The cell phone is a metaphor for the cultural dynamisms of globalization. What happens when social space becomes abstracted from physical space, when it becomes a matter of choice? What does this do to religion?

Religion in Globalized Space

Scholars of the cultural effects of globalization call the dynamic that I'm discussing *deterritorialization*. There are many versions of the concept, but the simplest defines it as the separation of social space from physical locale. Both good and bad come from the two dynamics we've uncovered with the cell phone. Globalization unbinds us from space and reduces us to individuals. Let's consider these in turn.

Globalization appears as a great force for cultural freedom. It frees us from the limits of our geographical and cultural locations. We all know this through the consumption of commercial popular culture ... to peek back at the iPod again. We listen to music from around the world, and American popular culture is full of elements lifted from others. We know this from more literal, physical consumption as well. My grandfather probably never tasted a mango. They are among my children's favorite foods. This has nothing to do with changing the part of the world we live in, and everything to do with how globalization has changed what it means to live in any part of the world. Marketing and migration have made us comfortable with and desirous of difference.

This same dynamic shows up in our religious communities. Local religious communities are unavoidably limited. Each is limited by the skills of its pastoral staff, limited by the focus of the shared elements of its traditions, limited by interests of its members. In the face of such unavoidable limits, globalization comes as a great liberator. You no longer have to move or go on pilgrimage to other religious sites or communities to find something different. The riches of the Christian and other world spiritual traditions are available at home. Add to this various community supplements such as on-line chat groups and parachurch organizations.

Together these provide enormously helpful supplements to the inevitable limits of local communities.

The globalizing effect of unbinding us from locality frees us in another genial way as well. It frees our moral imaginations to take in broader concerns. Globalization provides a great cosmopolitan opportunity for Christian concern. Just as my children love mangoes, they also feel concern for the victims of the recent tsunami in the Asian ocean. Their memories are apparently much longer than the media's—they continue to compete with each other at dinner prayers on the issue: the younger one trying to pray for the people hurt by the tsunami first, the older one keeping correct count of the earthquakes the same people have suffered since. This was very much an event that was experienced in a global manner. History has long known great natural disasters—from the great flood to the earthquake in Lisbon on All Saints' Day in 1755. These have spurred anguished religious and philosophical questioning from the Genesis accounts to Voltaire's *Candide*. But these events were learned of only secondhand, after the fact. The tsunami was experienced in real time as an ongoing disaster that demanded a response.

Here we see that globalization impacts more than imagination. It also provides greater opportunities for action. Within hours donation sites had been set up on the Internet to enable people to support relief and recovery efforts. The 1998 Synod of Catholic Bishops of the Americas described this cosmopolitan possibility as the "Globalization of Solidarity." They, along with John Paul II, embraced globalization as both a challenge and an opportunity for Christian discipleship. The document from that synod, *Ecclesia in America*, sketches the outlines of a spirituality for a globalized age: a global concern informed, guided, and sustained by belief in the Trinity and the mystical body of Christ.

But this positive potential is accompanied by the danger of this spirituality remaining an abstract ideal, a form of religious imagination that is unmoored from concrete practice, or realized only through very remote ones. Distant charitable actions, such as giving to tsunami relief efforts, for all their importance for those they help, require little engagement from us. Johann-Baptist Metz has called such monetary donations the "quasi-sacrament" of bourgeois Christianity. Certainly there is nothing wrong with making charitable donations. But as Metz observed, it is not a form of relationship that involves us deeply, that puts us at risk, that calls us to the "change of heart" that is the center of gospel spirituality.[3]

This is the hidden, fundamental spiritual and ethical challenge of globalization. How can we lengthen what Zygmunt Bauman has called the "powerful but short" arms of moral concern? Our moral traditions and sensibilities developed in a history of local communities. How can they be adapted to a global ethical sphere?[4] The globalization of solidarity offers us the opportunity to lengthen them, but I worry that this will result not in strength but in a great atrophy. We are bombarded by endless needs that we can do little to directly address. Occasionally an event will rise into media focus and thus collective consciousness and call forth a response. But the rest leave us in abstracted inaction, either nursing a spirituality of global concern that remains largely virtual or bearing the burden of generalized guilt that locks us into inaction.

This is the downside to the freedoms from locality that globalization brings. In addition to being freed, we are unbound in the sense of being disconnected, loosed from ties to any particular place, deprived of roots that bind our beliefs to practice, to a certain form of common life. This downside has long lurked within discussions of cosmopolitanism. If cosmopolitans are admired for the universal scope of their interests, they are also suspect for lacking particular commitments. At home in the world, they are tied to the fate of no place or people.

The importance of place was brought home to me by an action my parish took in response to the second round of President Bush's tax cuts. These arrived in the summer of 2003 in the form of substantial child tax credit rebate checks for middle-class families with children. Our parish is fairly progressive, so Catholic commitments to the common good still counter the antigovernment tide of contemporary politics. For this reason, many parishioners were opposed to the policy of tax cuts as a matter of principle. Those in the know were further disturbed by the fact that Congress did not proportionately increase the refundability of the tax credit, meaning that families with incomes less than $26,000—the working poor—received no checks. But such principles don't carry a whole lot of weight when a check for $800 arrives in the mail right around vacation time. The values are there, but the budget and deficits are so big, it all easily recedes into abstraction—precisely the problem at stake with global issues.

Place made the difference here. Our parish is made up of rich and poor, and thus of families who received checks and those who did not. The financially secure got a windfall, and those who were struggling to clothe and house their children got nothing. This place, this specific community allowed abstract principles of justice to appear in the concrete. Beliefs only function heuristically, as searchlights that illuminate history and human obligation, when they can be focused on a particular setting. It is in concrete human interactions that spiritualities of communion and solidarity can leave the virtual realm and be put into practice.

The tax rebates challenged the parish's attempts to be a Eucharistic community. They threatened to put the lie to laudable "multicultural" liturgies and other attempts to unite the various groups that constitute the parish. Within the context of the parish, in the face of parishioners left out, abstract policies became concrete, and many responded by saying "no" to a political order that shortchanged their poorer brothers and sisters. Eighty families responded by symbolically "reallocating" their refunds to charities that serve the common good. Some directly signed their checks over to poorer parish families that received none.

A second noteworthy aspect of this example is how it involved more than just the exchange of money. It provided the opportunity for parishioners to become personally aware of each other's lives. Directly sharing refunds with needier families began relationships that brought with them friendship, deeper understanding, and at times more challenging requests for help. Thus it provoked the change of heart Metz looks for in a way that donations to tsunami relief do not.

One lesson here is that face-to-face encounters bring about stronger responses than those that take place through the media. That is true, but it is not particularly helpful for responding to globalization since this will inevitably involve responses over vast distances. There is a more subtle point about place here that is helpful for responding to the challenges of globalization. Personal relations can ground, focus, and strengthen our response to large, abstract issues. And the parish or congregation, as a local community where beliefs are practiced, is a privileged place where this can happen.[5]

This is, of course, simply a variation on the venerable environmental dictum "Think globally, act locally"—but with a twist. Unlike environmental issues, not all global solidarity issues admit of local appearance and action. But church structures have the potential to create spaces where they are made present and actionable.

Think of the importance that Central America held for North American believers in the 1980s. Many North American churches helped resettle immigrants or offered sanctuary to undocumented exiles. This made distant issues concrete and personal and led to a political radicalization of many religious believers that has held firm for decades. The text of the Synod of the Americas speaks of intrachurch cooperation in the region, and this has proved powerful in the past. Note, however, how many of the most pressing global issues we currently face (e.g., Iraq, Darfur) have little local church mediation. Not surprisingly, American response to these remains rather abstract and virtual—dependent as it is on media presentation and lacking any direct means of action. Religious difference is an issue as well. The forging of interreligious solidarity is no doubt one of the most pressing issues we face in the twenty-first century.

There is another way in which globalization weakens as much as it liberates. As the cell phone example illustrates, it reduces us to individuals. This frees us to seek and form new associations with great flexibility. Thus the massive protests that preceded the invasion of Iraq depended on the new communication technologies. The Internet and e-mail enabled the mobilization of hundreds of thousands of people in a stunningly short period of time. It took years for the Vietnam antiwar movement to produce such numbers. But this rapid deployment seems to be accompanied by a lack of staying power.

Contrast this with the deep structures that undergirded the civil rights movement. Black churches provided an infrastructure robust enough to sustain a multigenerational struggle. The movement was composed not just of committed individuals but of communities where shared beliefs, mutual challenge, encouragement, and shared experiences could support involvement in a struggle that was inconvenient, demanding, and dangerous.

Responding in Faith and Courage

Consumer culture and globalization present both profound opportunities and profound challenges. On the plus side they make possible unprecedented access to the riches of traditions and they provide new opportunities for global awareness and action. But these opportunities can only be realized if their pitfalls are negotiated. Consumer culture and globalization are great dissolving and eroding forces. They separate religious traditions into disconnected, abstract collections of symbols, beliefs, and values. They disconnect beliefs from the forms of life that give them traction in the world. They unmoor us from the communities and spaces where they can be put into practice. While they bring individual freedoms, collectively they may reduce us to building only castles of sand that are unable to stand the riptides of contemporary global capitalism and terrorism or the gargantuan environmental and natural resource crises on the horizon.

Responding to these challenges will require both a reevaluation of previous strategies and the development of new ones. Progressives in particular must reevaluate their suspicions of institutions and frustrations with the shortcomings of traditions, which are by definition ongoing, unfinished realities. Indeed, religious institutions, with their hesitance and inertia, appeal more to the nostalgic imagination of conservatives than the utopian sensibilities of progressives. But in an ever-changing, fluid, globalizing world, they provide essential places to stand and from which to act. We need to realize the importance of these locations and struggle to protect the fullness of their supporting traditions from the fragmenting and constricting reductions of fundamentalism.

Reevaluating and working to preserve communal institutions and religious traditions is an odd sort of struggle. We face not some dictatorially imposed secularization but vast frictionless freedoms of choice. We face the same inevitable limits of communities, traditions, and institutions as our forebears. These limits are frustrating, and in our religious communities that can be profoundly painful. But unlike those before us, we are free simply to walk away and seek a separate peace. We do this either by literally abandoning our religious and other communities or by defecting in place and retreating into a personal spirituality, a private set of meanings unmoored from broader communal conversation and practice. Indeed, this is the particular temptation that consumer culture and globalization pose for progressives—a vast dissipation into a thousand disparate utopias, abandoning traditional spaces to conservatives.

A full response to the erosions of consumer culture and globalization requires a vast effort to ground faith in tradition, practice, and community. We must cultivate a sensitivity to connections: connections among symbols, beliefs, and values; connections between those and ritual and practices; connections between all of those and communities, institutions, and spaces. This amounts to a recovery of the full meaning of the word *spirituality* as a concrete form of life, guided by a spiritual vision, tied to transformative practices and concrete actions in particular spaces. Our local parishes and congregations still provide potent locations for living a graced life of engaged discipleship. Consumer culture and globalization call for a spirituality that will take these mundane local spaces seriously.

Globalization in particular calls for a spiritual vision that can see the whole world as a space of moral significance and that can connect global concern with local action. We should mine our communal traditions for their particular riches for making connections both on the local and global levels, both within the community and with those outside of it. Our rich religious traditions, practices, and structures support hospitality, communion, and solidarity, from our celebration of the Eucharist to our belief in the unity of all believers in the one Church of Christ, from prophetic concern for the poor and outcasts to hope in the destiny of all in the Kingdom of God. These are not simply beliefs, they are tied to a host of particular practices and institutions.

All of this brings to mind a passage from the talk Thomas Merton gave just before his death. He quoted a Tibetan abbot's message to a monk forced to flee the country as the Communists took over: "from now on, Brother, everybody stands on his own feet."[6] The twentieth century rightly taught us to question institutions and collectivism. And the twenty-first century's brief tenure hasn't offered much better evidence for what some of us term the "institutional" church. But the eroding and individualizing forces of consumer culture and globalization pose new challenges. We still need the spiritual virtues of courage, fortitude, and initiative embodied in the monk forced to flee alone. But Merton's message needs to be updated for a new age, one that was already coming to birth in his own. Sisters and brothers, we live in a society that constantly encourages us to imagine we stand alone. But the gospel transforms the world only when disciples stand together. The church, with all its frustrations and flaws, provides a place to stand and from which to act. In a world that offers us the easy out of a separate peace in our own private spirituality, the church is a place worth considering, devoting your life to, and yes, fighting for, not just for ourselves but for the generations to come.

Notes

1. Robert Bocock, *Consumption* (New York: Routledge, 1992), 118.

2. Robert MacMillan, "Test Your Personality, Digitally," *WashingtonPost.com*, April 18, 2005; Elisabeth Bumiller, "White House Letter: President Bush's iPod," *NYTimes.com*, April 11, 2005; Del Quentin Wilber, "IPod Devotees Rocked by Thefts," *Washington Post*, April 16, 2005, A01.

3. Johann-Baptist Metz, "Messianic or 'Bourgeois' Religion," in *Faith and the Future: Essays on Theology, Solidarity, and Modernity*, edited by Francis Schüssler Fiorenza (Maryknoll, N.Y.: Orbis, 1995), 22.

4. Zygmunt Bauman, *Postmodern Ethics* (Oxford: Blackwell, 1993), 218, discussed in John Tomlinson, *Globalization and Culture* (Cambridge: Polity, 1999), 198–207.

5. Not addressed here is how globalization erodes nation-states as places of effective political action for influencing domestic economies. This results in the decline of policy as a focus of political imagination and feeds the turn to "values" issues. Thus, globalization provides an important part of the answer to Thomas Frank's question in *What's the Matter with Kansas?* (New York: Metropolitan, 2004). See Zygmunt Bauman, *Globalization: The Human Consequences* (New York: Columbia University Press, 1998).

6. *The Asian Journal of Thomas Merton* (New York: New Directions, 1973), 338.

Putting Our Money Where God's Mouth Is: The Biblical Case for Economic Justice

GARRET KEIZER

Oppressing the poor in order to enrich oneself,
and giving to the rich, will lead only to loss.

—*Proverbs* 22:16

There is a time during the Eucharist as it's celebrated in many Christian churches called the offertory, and there was a time early in my tenure as an Episcopal priest when I found the offertory a bit awkward. This was when the ushers brought forward the money. Having duly set the Lord's table with a plate of dainty wafers and a chalice of diluted wine, centering both on an immaculate linen cloth, I would receive the loaded collection plate like a gross dish of four and twenty greenbacks baked in a pie, with a crumpled wing or two poking through the crust. A sort of table grace was said—"All things come of thee, O Lord, and of thine own have we given thee"—but then there was the problem of where to put the thing. Center stage didn't seem right, like having the prop mistress come out and blow her nose right next to the soprano. I tried to put the plate off to the side, though our altar was small and there was only so far I could shove it without pushing it over the edge. The dilemma was not necessarily unique to me. I've been in churches where the plate is ceremoniously waved over the table, presumably at the risk of stinking up the air, and then taken by a deacon or acolyte into the sacristy.

It may seem as though I'm dwelling on a minor liturgical detail, but I am in fact pointing to a heresy. Basically it boils down to a denial of the flesh. I was perhaps more orthodox in my preaching than in my sacramental gestures, for I sometimes told my parish that if "people of the book" were correct in believing that "God created the heavens and the earth," and if we Christians were correct in believing that "the Word became flesh and lived among us," then there were three subjects about which it was impossible to speak too often in church, those being sex, politics, and money—precisely those subjects that many people believe should never be mentioned there.

Of course, the scruple is entirely disingenuous. We relegate things to the sphere of the profane in the hopes of reserving them for ourselves. A dog pees on a hydrant, a teenager trashes his room, and an upstanding citizen regards politics as corrupt and money as corrupting for basically the same reason: to mark territory. The chief advantage of "filthy lucre" is that you can think of it as a thing too dirty to share with anyone else. You can skirt the issue of economic justice in the name of moral hygiene.

That has been the order of the day, not only in American religion but also in American politics, for a long time now. This includes so-called left-wing politics, which has increasingly become a politics of poses. The trick involves sticking your tongue out as provocatively as possible as an alternative to doing the same thing with your wallet or your neck. The result is our current conception of justice as a multicultural caste system wherein people of all races, creeds, colors, and sexual orientations eat dinner at a swanky restaurant while people of all races, creeds, colors, and sexual orientations eat dinner out of the garbage dumpster out back.

This is not to imply that important issues like cultural diversity are merely distractions from the cause of economic justice, only that those issues are inevitably demeaned by failing to take account of it. Environmentalism, for example, can begin to look a lot like keeping the peasantry out of his lordship's wood. Reproductive freedom translates, in a class system, to public policy at the level of a pimp: we slip some poor woman a few bills and tell her to "take care of it"—the very thing we refuse to do should she exercise her purported "right to choose" in a maternal direction. And let us not forget the lofty aim of having more authors of color on the syllabus, even as more and more children of color are deprived of the books. There's a word for all this, though people think you shouldn't say that in church either.

Even when we do speak of economic issues, we dress the wolf of class distinction in the sheep's clothing of sentiment. We romanticize the poor and demonize the rich. The moguls who own TV networks and motion picture studios seem only too happy to play along. That is because portraying the rich as abominably wicked allows us to go on believing that the *structures* that enable some people to get rich and others to live in squalor are fundamentally sound. If there were more cool guys who got rich, like Ben and Jerry, say, or Bill and Melinda, or Cheech and Chong, then we wouldn't need to change a thing. For the time being, best not to change a thing.

"Horses are not modest creatures," the novelist Robertson Davies once wrote in regard to the likelihood of sexual ignorance in an equestrian age. In regard to poverty and wealth, the Bible is not a modest book. It does not partake of our fastidiousness.

Almost as soon as the God of the Exodus makes himself known to the Children of Israel, he begins to lay down the law on economic justice. Those bound for the Promised Land are not allowed to take their creditors' clothing in pledge, to withhold their day laborers' wages until the following day, to reap the edges of their fields (reserved for the poor), or to lend money at interest. Of special concern to Yahweh are "widows and orphans," which in both the Old and New Testaments amount to synonyms for the destitute. We tend to hear the word *widow* and picture our old mum, but biblical widows are not necessarily old. Like Ruth before her, the Virgin Mary may soon have been one. The widow evinces the vulnerability of women in patriarchal cultures and the mortality of men in times of war. It takes no great leap to see the widow of the Bible as the working-class single mother of today. She, too, is a casualty of war, including cultural war. Her betters debate the big issues and she mops up the mess. They shift the paradigms at the conference and she fluffs the towels at the conferees' hotel.

The mandate for justice that we find in the Mosaic Law becomes nothing short of a passion in the prophets. One of the great travesties of the Christian Right is its restriction of biblical "prophecy" to the apocalyptic (and in their context, relatively eccentric) books of Daniel and Revelation. This is something like going to the Louvre to look at the carpeting. For something closer to the essence of biblical prophecy, consider the inspired herdsman Amos, speaking seven and a half centuries before the birth of Christ:

Thus says the Lord:
For three transgressions of Israel,
and for four, I will not revoke punishment;
because they sell the righteous for silver,
and the needy for a pair of sandals—
they who trample the head of the poor into the dust of the earth
and push the afflicted out of the way.

His contemporary Isaiah, prophesying to the south, sounds a similar note:

Ah, you who join house to house,
who add field to field,
until there is room for no one but you,
and you are left to live alone in the midst of the land!

Jesus is very much in this tradition when he inveighs against those who "devour widows' houses and for the sake of appearance say long prayers." So is James, leader of the Jerusalem church and "Brother of the Lord," when he closes his epistle by saying, "Come now, you rich people, weep and wail for the miseries that are coming to you.... The wages of the laborers who mowed your fields, which you kept back by fraud, cry out, and the cries of the harvesters have reached the ears of the Lord of hosts." Liberals find it ironic that right-wing demagogues can ignore passages like these in order to fixate on issues like gay marriage and the "right" of the brain dead to be put on exhibit as furlough entertainment for the Armies of Life. But this is not irony so much as strategy. It is a sleight of hand trick in which you are told to keep your eye on the gay groom—imagine a tux that color!—while the money disappears off the table once again.

Strictly speaking, there is no "biblical argument for economic justice" for the simple reason that, with the possible exception of a few New Testament epistles, the Bible does not argue. Its writers were not logicians. Nevertheless, one can construct a strong argument for economic justice based on certain premises that are central to the biblical understanding of the world.

The first is that human beings are members of the same family. The Bible believer says this is because God made us all and made us in God's image. The microbiologist says that the proof is in the DNA. At bottom the only solid common ground in the world is the recognition that we ourselves are the common ground, made of common clay, grown of common genes.

But the practical expression of this is neither biological nor theological but economic. "You were bought with a price," says St. Paul, speaking of the Atonement; but our common humanity is also certified "with a price." A poor relation whose family allows her to starve is in fact no longer a relation. This is not to say that "brotherhood" necessitates equality, but if brotherhood is to be anything better than a meaningless abstraction, it does require a certain parity. Different members of the same rock band may earn different salaries; the songwriter gets a royalty, and the founding guitarist may earn more than the new guy on drums. But if anyone's salary is not even in the same orbit as those of others in the band, then he is simply not "in the band." He's a studio musician or he's a chump, but you won't see his face on the album.

This principle is implicit throughout the Bible, even in some passages that strike us as barbaric. The book of Deuteronomy forbids the beating of malefactors in excess of forty lashes, "lest... thy brother should seem vile unto thee." Is it such an exegetical stretch to say that a worker's salary must not fall below a mandatory living wage for the same reason?

The second principle underlying the biblical imperative for economic justice is the interdependence of creatures. The law against working on the Sabbath includes servants, livestock, and "the alien resident in your towns" because it is understood that your Sabbath rest has in some ways been won by their labors. The Deuteronomic law that forbids muzzling an ox "while it is treading out the grain" rests on the same principle. When Paul says, "The eye cannot say to the hand, 'I have no need of you,'" he is thinking specifically of the church but with reference to all bodies, including the body politic. The organic nature of society means that our ledgers overlap. The oriental carpet lying in what used to be the boys' bedroom was partially paid for by the low wages of their childcare worker and the janitor for their dorm.

The third reason that economic justice is incumbent on the children of God is that economic injustice is a lie about reasons one and two. When a creature with the DNA of a human being lives the life of a dog, that is falsehood of the most egregious and blasphemous kind. If the devil is "the father of lies," then economic injustice is the devil's only begotten son.

Of course it can be argued that gross inequality is also expressive of a truth, since human beings exhibit widely divergent amounts of talent, initiative, and plain dumb luck. But even if we grant that inequality is natural to the human condition, and that "natural law" is the same as the law of the Bible (a much harder case to make), we would still be challenged by the math. The thresholds of genius and mental retardation stack up to an IQ ratio of about 140 to 70, or 2 to 1. The ratio of the average salary of a leading CEO to that of an American worker is running something like 431 to 1. The ratio of the lowliest billionaire's "worth" to that of a typical street person is 1,000,000,000 to 1/10 of 1. "Figures don't lie," but in the last two cases they do; they bear false witness against (the very nature of) our neighbor.

Finally, it needs to be said that truth in the biblical tradition is not simply a matter of factuality but of divine intention. When Jesus speaks of the "kingdom of God," he means a world in which the will of God is a done deal, "on earth as it is in heaven." When he meets a woman "bent over and... quite unable to stand up straight," Jesus does not speak of her condition as "the will of God" or "nature's way" of bringing her to God. He does not talk to her about the redemptive value of suffering. He refers to her as "this woman... whom Satan bound for eighteen long years" and heals her.

This refusal to say "Whatever is, is good" points to several, more subtle biblical arguments for economic justice. The Bible is often criticized for putting humanity above nature. A favorite verse with the critics is the one in Genesis where God tells humanity to "subdue" the earth. I, for one, think it is time for people of the Bible to plead guilty to the charge. And, if possible, to be held in contempt of court. Better that than speaking of destitution as just another culture within the Great Rainbow of Diversity or the role of human bottom feeder as just another niche in the Great Circle of Life. In regard to notions like these, I'd rather quote Bessie Smith than scripture: "Who ever heard of such shit?"

Equality is an entirely human construct, a defiance of "nature" no less than a recognition of our common nature. It is revealed religion holding natural theology in check. Walk in the woods and you'll get the point. The trees crowd one another for the light, and the small pines wither under the canopy of their taller neighbors. I have wondered if the idea of equality actually began with the cultivation of gardens (of Eden?) and orchards, when plants were first spaced so that each could receive its required measure of sunlight. Or perhaps equality began at the breast, when a mother of twins gave both of her babies an equal share of milk as opposed to letting the stronger suckling crowd out the weak. It is no surprise that the God of the prophets speaks of herself as a consoling mother and of Jerusalem as a place where "you shall drink deeply with delight from her glorious bosom." This is maternal imagery, to be sure, but it is hardly an evocation of Mother Nature.

Or of Dame Fortune. The Bible doesn't believe in luck. Until we get to the "elect" of the New Testament, it has no word for fate. Even prophecy can be overturned by the will of the living God, as we see in

Exodus, where God "repents," and in Jonah, where God does the same. This may in fact be one of the most revolutionary of the Bible's implications, for it challenges alike the presumptuous "destiny" of empires and the notorious fatalism of the poor. The latter is certainly understandable, for without the excuse of an unlucky star or the hope of a winning number the condition of poverty would be unendurable. But a belief in fate, including a belief in the righteous determinism of markets, is always a defense of the status quo. That is the meaning, or one of the meanings, of the contest between Moses and the Pharaoh's "wise men and sorcerers." Only when the power of fate and fortune is defeated can the fortunes of slaves be reversed.

Finally, the Bible argues against economic injustice and class inequality by the emphasis it gives to the present life. Caste systems make moral sense only within belief systems that include reincarnation. With multiple lives, justice becomes a problem of long division with untold numbers of digits to be carried and subtracted before the final quotient can be known. But if this life is the sum total of our mortality, then injustice has nowhere to hide. Murder is not a matter of pushing the restart button; it's a matter of pulling the plug. The Bible does not explicitly rule out the possibility of reincarnation (Hassidic Jews, for example, believe in it), but its predominating implication is that this life is pretty much the deal. In that case, poverty is a very raw deal indeed. Of course Christians, as well as Muslims and some Jews, can plead extenuating circumstances on the grounds of an afterlife. The poor will get theirs in the sweet by-and-by. The rich had better heed the warning of James. But the peace we make with injustice betrays our apostasy, for if we truly believed in heaven and hell and the Great Comeuppance, would we not share our wealth as equitably and quickly as we could? The great hypocrisy, to say nothing of the great irony, of the Christian plutocrat consists less of failing to listen to the prophets than of failing to believe in the life to come.

I can imagine such a plutocrat accusing me of equivocation. All of my arguments thus far, he or she would say, make the biblical case for charity. No one could deny that. But that is not the same thing as a case for altering the basic economic structures of society. A change of heart is one thing. But the "systemic change" these left-wingers are always harping about, that's a horse of a different color.

Its name is love—as in "Thou shalt love thy neighbor as thyself." To do that sincerely, I must love my neighbor in the same effectual terms as I love myself. When I buy myself a gift, I want precision. If I want the John Coltrane boxed CD set, I don't buy myself the Britney Spears single and say, "It's the thought that counts." Similarly, no right-wing conservative, newly diagnosed with a malignant tumor, says to the physician, "Now, Doc, let's not go throwing money at this thing, which is how your liberals approach every problem. Let's proceed with a bit of common sense and volunteer initiative. I recall when my grandmother back in Nebraska got the Big C, there wasn't any of this chemotherapy mumbo jumbo, none of this mollycoddling with pain killers all day and night. The ladies from the church all baked casseroles and they came and stood around her bed and listened to her scream. That's when people knew a thing or two about *values*."

More like: "I want state of the art, Doc. Whatever it takes. Whatever it costs. Let's take this thing to the mat." That means sophisticated, systemic, fully committed, and fully funded. Can it mean anything less if we intend to love the child stricken with the cancers of poverty and racism *as we love ourselves?*

To leave the welfare of the poor to the charitable ministrations of the good is basically to commend them to chance. Should St. Francis wander into their trailer park flush and in a good mood, they're in luck. Otherwise, too bad. The Good Samaritan, that patron saint of volunteers, makes this same point. True, the Samaritan is willing to work alone. Seeing the wounded man in the road, he is unwilling to see him as someone else's responsibility. He acts. But once he has bound the man's wounds and put him on his animal, he seeks help from an innkeeper and gives him money for the recovering man's care. The Samaritan refuses to see social action as anything other than a social activity, that is, one involving collective effort. He also refuses to see it apart from its economic cost. Seemingly the paragon of compassionate conservatives, the Good Samaritan turns out to be a tax-and-spend liberal! And he's the best sort of tax-and-spend liberal, because he starts with himself.

Conservatives balk at the idea of encoding compassion in public policy, preferring to rely on "traditional values," but in fact public policy rests on an idea no less traditional than that of original sin. Laws, policies, and programs are in effect admissions of human weakness. They are also expressions of collective strength—of our ability to bear one another's burdens, including the burden of our sin.

As an example, consider the very sensible law that states all motorists will stop when a school bus is loading or unloading children. Now my mother would stop for a school bus, law or no. In a state of total societal breakdown, zombies on the loose, Godzilla in the rearview mirror, my mother would still stop for the bus. Likewise, there are certain psychopaths who would try to run over children no matter what laws were in place. For most of us, though, it's a matter of good days and bad. If I'm late for work, if the coast looks clear, if there's no law that forbids me from doing otherwise, maybe I'll chance it. If there's a whole string of kids in the road, I'll probably stop. If one of the kids is mine, I'll probably jump out of the car and make sure that everybody else stops.

What good laws do, what progressive public policy does, is to make the best behavior of the best people on their best days normative for the society as a whole. We are not all like my mother, but we are able to choose, through the apparatus of our politics, to be as good as she is in the area of school bus safety. Our common life is such that we don't all have to be my mother in order to create a common way of life that is as safe and generous as it would be if we were. This is a lovely thing, in that it simultaneously tells the truth about our weakness (our "fallen nature," if you prefer) and our strength (that we are in the image of God, who according to Christians is a community of persons, Father, Son, and Holy Spirit).

To vote for a law that taxes my income with an eye to the creation of a more just commonwealth means that I can be as intentionally compassionate for 365 days of the year as I was on November 2, when I stepped into the booth somewhat more informed than I usually am and with the Feast of All Saints fresh in my mind. Think of it as lighting a votive candle. I'm not a Roman Catholic, but I rarely pass a Catholic church in the city without going in to light one, and lately I light it for the soul of my late, dear, and dissenting-Catholic friend Jimmy, who once explained to me what the candle thing was all about. "It's a symbol of your presence," he told me. "You're unable to remain by the image of the Blessed Mother for an hour, but your candle does, and in the mystery of your intention, it 'counts' as if you were there." A progressive law amounts to a candle I light in the privacy of a voting booth, where my left hand does not know what my right hand is doing, just as on most days I really don't know what I'm doing, though my political "presence" continues to "pray" in spite of all distractions.

If there are biblically derived arguments for economic justice, there are also biblically derived reasons against it. We are too cynical if we claim that the only reason people have for resisting a more equitable arrangement is the crass desire to hoard more wealth for themselves. After all, some of the people who would benefit most from revolutionary changes in our economic structures are those who resist those changes most vehemently. Indeed, the current American regime owes much to their vehemence.

First of all there is Jesus's often-quoted saying, "The poor you have with you always." It helps to know the context. Mary of Bethany anoints the head of Jesus with perfume and Judas Iscariot asks why the ointment was "wasted in this way," noting that it ought rather to have been sold "and the money given to the poor." Jesus replies "Let her alone . . . you always have the poor with you, and you can show kindness to them whenever you wish, but you will not always have me." As he is wont to do, Jesus is alluding to the Torah. "There will never cease to be some need on the earth."

And this may be so. Perhaps both Jesus and the Torah are saying that in any society, however well constructed, there will be individuals who sink to the bottom—or who sink lower than the projected bottom. If that is the case, then the poor are in fact icons of God, insolvable as God is. The grammar school atheist asks if God can make a rock so heavy that God himself cannot lift it. Perhaps the poor are that stone, a paradox as inscrutable as the Almighty. Perhaps this is the deeper meaning of that verse in Proverbs: "Those who mock the poor insult their maker."

But those who use Jesus's reply to Judas as some kind of proof text in support of injustice mock our intelligence. If the poor are with us always, that does not mean that the poor need always live in misery and squalor. Samuel Johnson said that a "decent provision for the poor is the true test of civilization." No less true a test is the perpetual struggle to redefine *decent*. That, too, is with us always.

On a deeper level, though, I believe that Jesus is challenging the very attitude that allows poverty to exist in the first place. Before you listen to Jesus, you have to listen to Judas. He reminds me of the small-town skinflint who votes down a school budget, saying he'd "just as soon see all this money go for a remedial-reading program or something like that." Of course if a fully funded remedial-reading program were put forward as a motion, he'd vote that down, too, but for now he uses it to define his unimpeachable high ground. Rather than give money to "bums on welfare," he'd "just as soon send it to hungry little kids in Africa"—but propose a bill for increased aid to Rwanda, and he'd "just as soon" turn his attention to the last tsunami. "Poor," or some variant thereof, is his way of saying "when dogs get wings." Or "after the revolution," as the case may be. In other words, the poor "are with us always" as an excuse not to relieve any form of neediness short of the Ultimate Need. This amounts to the most cynical form of exploitation: rhetorical exploitation. In that regard, Robert Frost spoke for the Judas in all of us when he said that we should not be too quick to advance the poor. "I need them in my business."

People also fear, or claim to fear, that the establishment of a more just economic order will somehow render the offices of neighborliness obsolete. The Good Samaritan will go the way of the Knights Templar and the poodle skirt. The milk of human kindness will sour unsipped in its glass. We will have gained the world and lost our souls.

But to believe this is already to have lost one's imagination. Can anyone honestly fear that we will ever succeed in abolishing suffering? We can ensure that everyone is able to ride the train, we can unionize the conductors and abolish the first-class compartment, but a child will still occasionally get crushed under the wheels. I trust that there will be Good Samaritans in Paradise, not only because they will deserve to be there but also because they will have work to do, albeit of an especially delicious kind.

Finally, and I have to say most incredibly, there is the "religious" fear of "materialism." Supply every need for the body, and no one will care for the soul. This is a bit like fearing that a diet is going to make you fat. The enemy of the spirit is not justice but surfeit. When everyone has enough, but hardly anyone has more than enough, we become more human. It is when serfdom is abolished, and bourgeois privilege is held in check, that people are able to explore the natural aristocracy of the unencumbered human being. I am told that greenhouses flourished during the Great Depression. Public libraries were packed. Tell me that this represents a lower degree of culture than shopping malls and Hooters-type vomitoriums. This is not an argument for soup lines and falling stock prices. It is rather an argument for everyone having some soup and everyone having title as a shareholder. And for young women having better opportunities than a second job at Hooters.

The sooner a society meets its members' material needs, the faster it fosters their spiritual growth; that is, the faster it brings them to the limitations of the purely material. Which of the "major religions" grew up in response to starvation? People struggling to survive may beg the bounty of the gods, but they seldom give themselves to the contemplative life. The voluntary "poverty" of monastic orders East and West is actually devoid of the most salient feature of poverty: uncertainty about the material future. No Franciscan mendicant seriously worries about where he'll sleep for the night or what he'll eat. He can reap the spiritual benefits of "doing without" precisely because he knows that, on the grittiest level, he will never do without.

I hear America singing, or at least I hear conservative America singing: "It is not the business of government to make people happy." My own heart sings the same song. I don't believe it is the business of government to make people happy either. I believe it is the height of impertinence to presume that it can or even should. How do you know what will make me happy, and what makes you so sure that I want to be?

The business of government is to create the conditions that make happiness possible. The business of government is to eliminate those conditions that make people miserable. This is an implicitly biblical distinction. You cannot deduce what will make me happy from the Golden Rule. But you can, by using that measure, quite accurately deduce the conditions that thwart happiness. A lobster dinner will not make me happy if I'm allergic to shellfish, but hunger will make me unhappy no matter what I like to eat. Your own belly teaches you that.

"Surely, this commandment that I am commanding you today is not too hard for you," says God in the book of Deuteronomy, "nor is it too far away. . . . No, the word is very near to you; it is in your mouth and in your heart for you to observe." It is within reach, in other words, and I think that economic justice is as well. The components are virtually self-evident.

1. *National health insurance.* Jesus went about the villages healing people of their diseases. If Jesus manifests the will of God on earth, then the will of God is for people to be well. Thus to deny people medical care is to withhold God's benediction. In principle we already acknowledge this. The hospital emergency room turns no one away. In practice, however, we give any number of working people (45 million at present) a choice between wholeness and bankruptcy.

2. *Equality of educational opportunity.* Nothing in our society be-

speaks our peace with injustice more than the ease with which we assume that "nice communities" will have "nice schools" and "bad" ones won't. We can protest with the usual cant—money doesn't guarantee educational quality and Lincoln went to a one-room schoolhouse and my uncle went straight from an Appalachian hill town to Harvard Medical. Yes, and your grandmother smoked four packs of cigarettes a day and lived to ninety-six. It happens, "shit happens," but happenstance is not policy. The bottom line for most Americans is that the school you attend reflects the economic well-being of the community in which you live, and the education you receive in turn determines the standard of living you will enjoy. Even within individual schools, tracking and lumping by ability level serve to guarantee that people will know their place. "Class" is what you take and class is what you learn. Like the church, a just educational system will be "one, holy, catholic, and apostolic," by which I mostly mean that it will "own all things in common," including the budget.

3. *Work as the cornerstone of economic value.* Money earned through labor must enjoy a higher status, and a lower rate of taxation, than money earned through the manipulation of money. Perhaps it is not possible or desirable to eliminate the concept of lending for interest, though if people eager to enact every sexual prohibition in Leviticus were as zealous to apply Torah economically, we could not do otherwise. But it is possible, desirable, and from any conceivable religious point of view obligatory to treat usury as nothing more than a necessary evil and labor as nothing less than a sanctified good.

4. *A reduction of the gap between rich and poor.* It is now greater than at any time since the Great Depression, with 1 percent of the population owning 40 percent of the national wealth. "Whoever has two coats must share with anyone who has none," says John the Baptist. George Orwell, who is chiefly remembered as a critic of totalitarian Socialism and chiefly forgotten as a lifelong Socialist, wrote in 1941 (in his essay "The Lion and the Unicorn") that "the highest tax-free income in Britain [should] not exceed the lowest by more than ten to one," adding, "A

man with £3 a week and a man with £1,500 a year can feel themselves fellow creatures, which the Duke of Westminster and the sleepers on the Embankment benches cannot." I defer to any disinterested economist who can prove Orwell's ratio unworkable, but I find it useful for imagining what *might* work. Imagine, for instance, a minimum wage of $50,000 per year and a maximum of $500,000. Can we honestly say that a two-income household earning $1 million annually would not be able to enjoy a luxurious life or find sufficient incentives for getting out of bed in the morning? If so, then "shades of 1984" is the least of our worries. Try shades of *Gulliver's Travels,* with particular attention to the Yahoos.

5. *The abolition of homelessness and hunger.* These need to be seen as "cruel and unusual punishment," even for the "crimes" of substance abuse or intractable laziness. As for the "crime" of being born to lazy or addicted parents, there should be no punishment at all. Barbaric societies punish the children of offenders, selling them into slavery, executing them along with their parents. A society that permits children to be condemned because of their parentage lives on the border of barbarism. As long ago as the prophet Ezekiel (circa 570 BCE), the Bible rejected the idea that children's teeth should be "set on edge" because their parents had "eaten sour grapes." It is time to catch up with Ezekiel.

6. *Aid to poor countries.* The parable of the Good Samaritan is occasioned by someone asking Jesus, "Who is my neighbor?" His answer defies all bounds. We do not need to be as robust as Jesus in our definitions to arrive at a position of comparable liberality. Common sense will suffice. If we live in total isolation from the world, then perhaps our neighbors are Canada and Mexico. But if the sun never sets on our markets or our military bases, then the neighbors we are commanded to love "as ourselves" are quite literally everywhere. "God so loved the world" and so, it seems, must we.

This is a lot to ask, though perhaps not too much for a nation that can afford to spend between $2 billion and $4 billion a year on pornography and $116 billion on booze. Amos says: "Let justice roll down like waters, and righteousness like an ever-flowing stream." His is a different type of hydrology from trickle-down economics. Some churches hold that baptism may be done by "sprinkling," but the justice of the kingdom of God demands nothing short of full immersion.

With all due respect to those pioneering feminists who made it their motto, I have never been able to completely buy the idea that "the personal is the political." If the personal can be anything other than the personal, then, personally, I don't give a damn for it. You can have it.

I do believe, though, that the personal informs the political in the sense that our political convictions begin with our desires, that they are driven by our desires, and that when they become torpid, they can be revitalized by our becoming reacquainted with our desires. And I think this is true of religious convictions as well. Huston Smith said that Hinduism starts off by asking the question of what we want. If Smith was right, then I advocate beginning every discussion from the point of view of a Hindu.

Chalk it up to Christian perversity if I end this essay as I perhaps ought to have begun it: by asking myself what I desire. On the deepest level, what do I want?

It is bunk to say that I want justice. I want justice to the same degree of commitment that people who watch Fox News want truth. If I say I want justice, then I am claiming that in the depths of my heart the political has become the personal. It hasn't. I wish this essay would change the world, but more than that, I wish I were getting paid more to write it. I wish I were writing it in a villa overlooking the Adriatic Sea.

It is also bunk to say that I want to live in greater solidarity with the mass of humankind. In a passage from "Self-Reliance" in which Emerson chides himself for "the wicked dollar" he sometimes gives as charity to "such men as do not belong to me and to whom I do not belong," he goes on to write: "There is a class of person to whom by all spiritual affinity I am bought and sold; for them I will go to prison if need be." I know exactly what he means. The persons with whom I feel myself in deepest solidarity are persons deeply suspicious of words like *solidarity*

—of mass culture, mass production, and mass movements of all kinds. I am talking about people who do their jobs and expect other people to do the same, who read constantly and believe about half of what they read, who keep their voices down in hotel corridors and their hands to themselves at parties, which they attend only when no creditable lie or fortuitous broken bone can get them off. If sentiments such as these count as solidarity with the masses, then you may call me Che.

So what do I want? Do I even know? (You can pose that second question, by the way, only if you're fairly well-off. The hungry, the disenfranchised are condemned always to know what they want.) I think that I do. I should like to have what I will call one honest drink before I die. The condemned man's last request—though I'd prefer to make it in the absence of condemnation—that is what I want. I want to sit or stand at my ease and drink a prime vintage, a premium beer, and I want to drink it in such a way that I savor every swallow. I want to drink it knowing that there isn't a woman or man alive on the earth who can't have the same drink I'm having, not a child under all the phases of the moon who isn't vaccinated, educated, ice-creamed, and good-night kissed, and I want to know all of that with such assurance that for the time it takes me to finish my drink I don't need to have a thought for anything or anyone but the glass in my hand and the person I've chosen to have at my table —though what could be a lovelier thought or a more stimulating topic of conversation than the world I have just described, the pride and joy of all humankind.

That is what I want. And I'm not sure, to tell you the truth, if I would be drinking that drink in a bar or in a church, in heaven or "on earth as it is in heaven," or if, on the deepest level of my desire, there is any difference.

Acknowledgments

I owe an obvious debt of gratitude to the contributors to this volume, each of whom responded readily and enthusiastically to my invitation to be part of this project and each of whom then had to endure the inevitable pushing and pulling over format, approach, deadlines, and all the other laborious aspects of producing a book.

I am also indebted to Beacon's Amy Caldwell, who brought her own sure judgment to bear at critical junctures while also demonstrating a willingness to let herself be persuaded by differing views. There is no person more precious on God's earth than a publisher who is able to say, "Let me think about it."

My colleague Rita Nakashima Brock, coauthor of the pathbreaking *Proverbs of Ashes* and also codirector of the new Faith Voices Institute for the Common Good, deserves many thanks and much credit for planting the original idea for this volume back in December 2004.

I count myself very lucky to have been involved through the years in two faith communities that live out God's extravagant welcome in remarkable ways: Judson Memorial Church in New York City and All Saints Episcopal Church in Pasadena. Day in and day out—not just on Sundays—these congregations express the heart of the gospel in the peace and justice work they do and in the warm hospitality they radiate.

Finally, I wish to thank Progressive Christians Uniting and in particular its cofounders, John Cobb and George Regas, for encouraging me to come out to California and join them in a bolder corporate proclamation of the inclusive love of God. In these scoundrel times in America I cannot conceive of more important work to be doing or better companions to be doing it with.

Acknowledgments

About the Contributors

REV. CHLOE BREYER is associate minister at St. Mary's Episcopal Church in West Harlem. She serves on the steering committee of Episcopalians for Global Reconciliation and is the author of *The Close: A Young Woman's First Year at Seminary.* Chloe Breyer writes frequently for *Slate Magazine* and has contributed to *What One Person Can Do,* a forthcoming book about global poverty and the Millennium Development Goals. She lives in New York with her husband and two children.

SR. JOAN CHITTISTER, OSB, is a best-selling author and well-known international speaker on women in church and society, human rights, and peace and justice issues. She is the author of thirty books, including *Called to Question: A Spiritual Memoir* and *Scarred by Struggle, Transformed by Hope.* Chittister cochairs the Global Peace Initiative of Women Religious and Spiritual Leaders, a United Nations partner organization facilitating a worldwide network of women peace builders. A longtime writer for the *National Catholic Reporter,* Chittister now also produces a weekly column—"From Where I Stand"—for NCR's Web site. Joan Chittister also created Benetvision, a resource and research center for contemporary spirituality.

GARRET KEIZER is the author of five books: *No Place But Here: A Teacher's Vocation in a Rural Community, A Dresser of Sycamore Trees: The Finding of a Ministry, God of Beer* (a novel), *The Enigma of Anger: Essays on a Sometimes Deadly Sin,* and, most recently, *Help: The Original Human Dilemma.* Keizer is a frequent contributor to *Christian Century, Mother Jones,* and the *Village Voice*; he is also a contributing editor for *Harper's Magazine.* Keizer lectures at colleges and universities across the country on the subjects of community, faith, and vocation. Before turning to write full-time, he worked as a teacher of English in a public high school for fifteen years and as a rural Episcopal minister and priest for twenty-two years. Garret Keizer lives in northeastern Vermont with his wife, Kathy. They have one daughter, now in college.

REV. JAMES M. LAWSON, JR., is best known for his extraordinary role in the modern civil rights movement. In the early 1950s he found himself on the same road to discovering the immense social and spiritual power of nonviolent direct action as Rev. Martin Luther King, Jr. Lawson became Dr. King's mentor in nonviolence and also became the preeminent teacher of nonviolent direct action to the young leaders of the Student Nonviolent Coordinating Committee—leaders who would go on to take the civil rights movement deeper and farther. James Lawson is a United Methodist minister who continues to preach and teach nonviolence as president of the Southern Christian Leadership Council in Los Angeles.

PATRICK McCORMICK received his doctorate in moral theology from Rome's Gregorian University. He is professor of religious studies at Gonzaga University in Spokane, Washington. McCormick is the author of *Sin as Addiction* and *A Banqueter's Guide to the All Night Soup Kitchen of the Kingdom of God*. He is coauthor of *Character, Choices, and Community: The Three Faces of Christian Ethics* and *Facing Ethical Issues: Dimensions of Character, Choice, and Community*. Patrick McCormick has written dozens of articles and chapters on Christian and Catholic social ethics; for the past decade, he has published a monthly column on Christianity and culture for *U.S. Catholic*.

BILL McKIBBEN is now a scholar in residence at Middlebury College in Middlebury, Vermont. McKibben is the author of many books, including *The End of Nature* and *Wandering Home: A Long Walk across America's Most Hopeful Landscape*. He is a frequent contributor to *Harper's Magazine*, which first published the essay appearing in this collection. In *Harper's* it was published under the title "The Christian Paradox: How a Faithful Nation Gets Jesus Wrong" in August 2005.

VINCENT MILLER is associate professor of theology at Georgetown University, where he teaches courses in Catholic theology as well as religion and culture. Miller's research focuses on the question of tradition as a process: how religious belief is handed down through and across cultures. Miller's much-admired recent book, *Consuming Religion,* considers the ways in which consumer culture transforms religion and practice. He is now beginning work on a similar consideration of the religious effects of globalization.

CHED MYERS is an acclaimed biblical scholar and activist theologian who leads Bartimaeus Cooperative Ministries (www.bcm-net.org), headquartered in Southern California. BCM offers "Word and World" intensive training seminars throughout this country and abroad. Ched Myers is the author of numerous books and articles, including, most recently, *The Biblical Vision of Sabbath Economics.*

REV. HEIDI NEUMARK is the pastor of Trinity Lutheran Church (ELCA), which is located in a multiclass, multiracial, and multicultural neighborhood of Manhattan. For nineteen years prior to this assignment she was the pastor of Transfiguration Lutheran Church in the South Bronx. Her experiences in congregational and community ministry there led to a well-received book, *Breathing Space: A Spiritual Journey in the South Bronx,* which was published by Beacon Press. Rev. Neumark is married to Gregorio Orellano; they are the parents of two children.

REV. VIVIAN DENISE NIXON is a criminal justice advocate who directs the College and Community Fellowship at the City University of New York. She is an ordained minister of the African Methodist Episcopal Church and currently serves as associate minister at the Mount Olive AME Church in Port Washington, New York. Rev. Nixon has been honored for her passionate advocacy by the Correctional Association of New York and Rural Opportunities, Inc. She is the recipient of a Soros Justice Fellowship from the Open Society Institute. Her two-year fellowship project, called "Re-Enter Grace," commenced in August 2005. Vivian Nixon is also completing a book based upon her experiences, which will be titled *Guilty and Saved: Revelations of a Previously Incarcerated Preacher Woman.*

MARILYNNE ROBINSON was awarded the 2005 Pulitzer Prize for her novel *Gilead*, published by Farrar, Straus and Giroux. In 1981 her modern classic, *Housekeeping*, won the PEN/Hemingway Award. Marilynne Robinson is also the author of two important books of nonfiction, *Mother Country* and *The Death of Adam*. She teaches at the University of Iowa Writers' Workshop.

REV. ALEXIA SALVATIERRA is executive director of Clergy and Laity United for Economic Justice (CLUE), which is widely considered the strongest and most effective religion and labor coalition in the nation. CLUE, together with the Los Angeles Alliance for a New Economy, organized the grassroots campaign that thwarted the Wal-Mart Corporation's plans to build a SuperCenter in the low-income community of Inglewood, California. Ordained in the Lutheran (ELCA) tradition, Rev. Salvatierra also serves on the governing board of the national Faith and Public Life Resource Center in Washington, D.C.

REV. BILL SINKFORD is president of the Unitarian Universalist Association, which is headquartered in Boston. Over the past five years, Bill Sinkford's leadership has put the UUA on the front lines of an emerging coordinated faith-based challenge to the Bush administration's policy of militant "full-spectrum dominance" in international relations. He has also continued to invite Unitarian Universalist congregations to take forward positions in state, local, and national efforts to secure equal rights for lesbian, gay, bisexual, and transgendered Americans.

REV. RICK UFFORD-CHASE is the moderator of the 216th General Assembly of the Presbyterian Church USA. He is also the founder and international director of BorderLinks, a binational educational and community service organization staffed by a team of twenty-five Mexican and U.S. nationals. Ufford-Chase is a cofounder of the "No More Deaths" movement, which invites people from across the United States to come to the border to work in support of migrants who risk their lives crossing the desert. As the chief elected officer of a major Protestant denomination, Ufford-Chase is reaching out to the next generation of Presbyterian leaders and promoting new efforts to move Presbyterians out of the pews and into the world. Rick Ufford-Chase is married to Kitty Ufford-Chase, a lifelong Quaker who serves with the Tucson-Pima Women's Commission in southern Arizona. They are the parents of Teo, aged nine.